TRUST ME

LEARNING TO TRUST THAT GOD IS GOOD AND IN CONTROL EVEN WHEN LIFE IS DIFFICULT

Verna Birkey

Adapted by Claire McCarey and Heather Craig

REDEMPTION
PRESS

Published by Redemption Press, PO Box 427, Enumclaw, WA 98022
Toll-free (844) 2REDEEM (273-3336)

Redemption Press is honored to present this title in partnership with the author. The views expressed or implied in this work are those of the author. Redemption Press provides our imprint seal representing design excellence, creative content, and high-quality production.

Unless otherwise noted, all Scriptures are taken from the Holy Bible, New Living Translation, copyright © 1996, 2004 by Tyndale Charitable Trust. Used by permission of Tyndale House Publishers, Wheaton, Illinois 60189. All rights reserved.

Scripture References marked NIV are taken from the Holy Bible, New International Version®, NIV®. Copyright © 1973, 1978, 1984, 2011 by Biblica, Inc.™ Used by permission of Zondervan. All rights reserved worldwide. www.zondervan.com

Scripture references marked KJV are taken from the King James Version of the Bible.

Scripture references marked NASB are taken from the New American Standard Bible, © 1960, 1963, 1968, 1971, 1972, 1973, 1975, 1977 by The Lockman Foundation. Used by permission.

Scripture quotations marked ESV are taken from The Holy Bible: English Standard Version, copyright © 2001, Wheaton: Good News Publishers. Used by permission. All rights reserved.

ISBN 13: 978-1-68314-792-3
ePub ISBN: 978-1-68314-793-0
Kindle ISBN: 978-1-68314-794-7

Library of Congress Catalog Card Number: 2018963243

RECOMMENDATIONS
FOR *TRUST ME*

Claire and Heather have done us all a great service by updating Verna Birkey's book! Western Christians, steeped in a self-focused and self-entitled culture, desperately need a more robust theology of suffering. And the heart of a robust theology of suffering is the biblical teaching about God's goodness and sovereignty. Birkey's teaching on this truth is biblical, practical, and compassionate. May it receive a wide reading!

—Gary DeLashmutt
Co-Founder of Xenos Christian Fellowship in Columbus, Ohio
Author of
Loving God's Way: A Fresh Look at the One Another Passages and Colossians: Christ over All; Christ in You

Trust Me took biblical truth I have known in bits and pieces from over fifty years of faith and put them all together in one place. In reading it, I was reminded again not just why I can trust Jesus in times of hardship and struggle, but who it is I am trusting and what trusting Him looks like. The updates bring timeless truth into a current context, which made what I already know new again. It is also a book filled with empathy, which is rare. The stories represent different types of difficulties, with no weight or scale assigned to any. I consider it a resource for the Christian life that I will go back to again and again. I would feel comfortable sharing this with a new mom worn out from lack of sleep and a friend in despair over a tragic loss—it would be powerful and appropriate for both.

—Elizabeth Murphy, Speaker and Author

Far more important to Him than giving us an easy life is the development of our character and our growth in grace. Every person and event that enters our lives moves toward that one all-consuming passion of His heart, that we be like His Son. This declaration from the book conveys, for me, the essence of its message. With appropriate Scriptures, relevant stories, and simple but insightful questions, the reader is encouraged along the path of beneficial self-reflection to hopefully see the eternal purposes of God within the often confusing and painful experiences of life. This book may well function at its best when used as part of a structured group activity.

—Ian Stewart
Team Leader, Christian Guidelines Counseling Agency, Northern Ireland

"Trust Me" is not so much a command as an invitation to find our identity and rest in the One who is completely trustworthy. I envision people gathered around a living room to consider together what Claire and Heather have presented as a case for living under the banner of the One who is good and who is in control, and determining together that He is indeed at work in all the craziness of this life in a broken world. What hope we have as we lean into Him! The thoughtful questions provided allow for consideration of God's character and nature individually as well as corporately and compel us to respond to His goodness.

At a critical juncture in my life while facing the despairing loss of an infant son, God offered me hope with these words: "Now is the time to reconcile how you feel with what you know to be true." In a real way, that is the message of *Trust Me*. It is true that He is good and is in control, and that is our source of hope.

—Donna Crum
Speaker and Leadership Team Member of Park Community Church,
Chicago, Illinois

Where is God in this? How can God let this happen? How can God have control over this situation and still be good? These questions, and many versions of them, rumble beneath the surface in our sufferings and can erupt in anxiety, distress, despair, hopelessness, and guilt. In short, accessible chapters, this book seeks to address such questions biblically. There is no dodging of hard issues, and with the help of personal stories, we are repeatedly brought back to the best and most basic of responses: Trust Me. This book will help us personally and will also be useful in one-to-one discipling and small-group study. May the Lord use it widely to help us grow . . . in trusting Him.

—Dr. Andrew Collins
Consultant Psychiatrist and Executive Committee Member,
Biblical Counseling, UK

ABOUT THE AUTHOR

Verna Birkey, author of the original version of this book, *If God Is in Control, Why Is My World Falling Apart?*, is a woman before her time. For over thirty years she ministered worldwide to thousands of women through the Enriched Living Workshops, and she had a wonderful gift of applying truth to family life and everyday issues. She taught practical, biblical, timely messages spoken with authority and clarity and given by God.

Verna is a graduate of Goshen College, Indiana, and Columbia International University Graduate School, South Carolina, and is the author of thirteen books. Today she is a youthful ninety-year-old with an infectious and vibrant energy. Still driving, she continues to serve God and others as she visits residents in local care homes, bringing them the comfort and presence of God.

This book, now updated for a wider audience, seems even more relevant than when it was first written in 1990. It is filled with timeless truths and a strong message of hope and confidence in our uncertain world. Although theologically honest, her writing touches the heart.

Verna Birkey's name will stand alongside men and women of great faith. Her legacy to the body of Christ is immeasurable.

FOREWORD

A few years ago we were looking for some material on anxiety to use in our women's Bible study groups. Claire's mum pulled this old green book with curled-down corners from her bookshelves and suggested we try it. And so we read *If God Is in Control, Why Is My World Falling Apart?* for the first time, and we knew that our groups needed the contents of this book.

We ordered copies (secondhand, because the book was out of print) for the women in our groups. We met together in our small groups, poring over verses we had read—often for the first time—and were overwhelmed with truths God used to speak directly into all our circumstances. As He enlarged our understanding of His love for us, and as He strengthened our faith with an even bigger view of who He is, we knew that more people needed to have access to this book. And not just women! We knew the men in our church also needed to learn these truths.

Through the very humble and gracious Pam Johnston, we contacted Verna and, with great brazenness, asked if we could produce a new version of her book. The goal was to make this book available to anyone, whether they were new in their faith or had been walking with God for many years.

To our delight, Verna said yes! Thus began a five-year process of squeezing in time on the book between being mums and wives and workers and church leaders.

But now we are done, with a great deal of help and support from many people, including our Belfast Collective family, our husbands, Pam Johnston, and, of course, Verna.

We have two quick pieces of advice (there's that brazenness again!).

First, we encourage people to do this material in small groups rather than on their own. Working out how to understand and apply God's truth is a more challenging, enriching, and fulfilling experience when you get to participate with other people who want this too.

Second, there are questions at the end of each chapter to help with personal reflection and facilitate group discussion, but we would also recommend taking the time to work through the "Going Deeper" questions at the back of the book. One of the things we loved about this book was the time spent in different parts of God's Word, so we encourage you to take the time to do that. It will be worth it!

One final word. This book is not meant to be an exhaustive study of suffering or God's sovereignty. The goal of this book is that anyone reading might see more clearly how the Bible reveals to us a God who loves us, a God who is good, and a God who is in control. This is our prayer for you as you read it.

Claire and Heather

TABLE OF CONTENTS

INTRODUCTION

If you are reading this book, perhaps you have questions about God.

Maybe you are experiencing painful circumstances that threaten to shake your faith and cause you to doubt God's love. Perhaps you have a family member with cancer, or someone in your family has lost their job. Maybe you are experiencing a marriage breakdown or you have bills that can't be paid.

If you are reading this book, perhaps you just don't understand why people can believe in God when the world is so messed up.

The Bible gives us two significant, sustaining, and comforting truths for all the circumstances we face: God is good, and God is in control.

But when flights are delayed, when the baby won't sleep, when our plans fall through, when illness strikes, or when jobs are insecure, we feel as if everything is out of control . . .

Then the questions come flooding in. Why is this happening? What will the outcome be? What should I do now? How can I cope? These questions are normal, but underlying all the questions, we can have a deep-seated assurance that God is in control. Our lives, with their inconveniences and difficulties, have not taken Him by surprise.

In this time of staggering changes in our world, it is good to affirm that our loving Lord reigns over all the earth. It is even more comforting to know and believe that God rules in the daily circumstances of my personal life. Nothing in this world is out of His control. Life is different when I affirm that God is ruling in my current situation.

In all of this, what can bring us to a place of trust during large or small crises, when we feel our world is falling apart?

That is what this book is all about.

CHAPTER 1

God Knows Best

Rightly understood and accepted with the heart, the truth of God's loving control, coupled with a deep assurance that He actually cares for me, is one of the most peace-producing concepts in all of Scripture. But what can bring us to that place of trust?

THE CIRCLE OF GOD'S WILL

The above circle represents the sphere of God's will: God's way for us, His plan for our lives. And we will also include in this what He allows to happen to us in life—His permissive will. The *X* inside the circle represents the person whose basic life direction is to go God's way. He or she is committed to Jesus Christ as Savior, knows Him as Lord and Master, and wants to follow in His way.[1]

If our desire is to follow the way of God, to live in agreement with Him and have His will fulfilled in us, then that *X* represents you and me. We have responded to God's call to us through Paul when he said:

Therefore, I urge you, brothers and sisters, in view of God's mercy, to offer your bodies as a living sacrifice, holy and pleasing to God—this is your true and proper worship. Do not conform to the pattern of this world, but be transformed by the renewing of your mind. Then you will be able to test and approve what God's will is—his good, pleasing and perfect will. (Rom. 12:1–2 NIV).

At the end of Paul's life, he was able to say, "As for me, my life has already been poured out as an offering to God. The time of my death is near. I have fought the good fight, I have finished the race and I have remained faithful" (2 Tim. 4:6–7). Paul had lived his life with a single-minded purpose, with a solid commitment to walk in the ways of God and in the plans God had for him, and Paul's decision is one that every follower of Christ must make every single day, in every circumstance of life.

The desire to walk in God's way is the same attitude Jesus had and expressed in so many ways in the book of John: "For I have come down from heaven to do the will of God who sent me, not to do my own will" (John 6:38), and "I always do what pleases him" (John 8:29).

Jesus single-mindedly walked in God's ways as God revealed them step by step. The supreme expression of this commitment came during those closing days of His life and the trying hours in the garden of Gethsemane as He poured out His heart to the Father to "take this cup of suffering away from me." But when the cup remained, His sincere and unqualified prayer continued to be "I want your will to be done, not mine" (Luke 22:42).

COMMITTED TO GOD'S WILL

For us, the first mile of the journey toward peace is this same commitment to the will of God that Jesus had, and like Jesus, we must be committed to choosing God's will above our own will, above our own preferences, and above our own desires.

God's ultimate and general will for all of His children is that we become more and more Christlike, that we increasingly become "conformed to the image of his Son" (Rom. 8:29 NIV). In addition, He promises to lead each of us in the way we should go. As we trust in His will, we can be sure He will direct us on our specific path. He directs us in many ways. For example, He directs us through the Bible, through the voice of circumstances, or through the advice of a trusted, godly friend. He may use other means, but one thing is sure: God never guides us into sin, nor does He ever expect us to do anything contrary to His Word.

GOD'S GOOD, PLEASING, AND PERFECT WILL

It is reassuring and encouraging to know that what God wills for us is what's best for us. His will is "good, pleasing, and perfect." However, many of God's children tend to have a wrong view of His will. Perhaps they think it is difficult, harsh, or against their best interests. Some may think God is out to make their lives miserable and take away all those things, people, or even ministries in which they find joy. But our loving heavenly Father is not like that. John 10:10 NIV says, "I have come that they may have life, and have it to the full." As He promises us in this verse, He is interested in our personal welfare and our best interests. The love God has for us is wrapped up in His goodness, and His posture toward us is always one of love and doing what is best for us. Numerous times in Deuteronomy the promise comes "that it may be well with you." This was God's heart for His people then and is still true for us today.

Jess's Story: *I became a Christian at a young age, and growing up, I increasingly wanted to live for God. Somewhere along the way, however, my thinking got a bit confused. I began to see God's will as a tightrope and almost impossible to discern. I believed that God would always ask me to give up what I wanted for something less desirable. His will for me would always be more painful or more difficult. By giving up what I wanted and accepting a harder path, I could prove my love to Him and learn the most about service and devotion. This belief came from right intentions, but it led to months and months of worry and confusion. Was I studying the right subjects? Was I in the right relationship? This led to a long period where I couldn't even pray. I couldn't come before God until I was sure I was in His will.*

GOD DOES KNOW BEST

Many of us can identify with these sentiments. In fact, it is true that we scarcely think that God, our Father, is equal to us in tenderness, love, and thoughtful care. Often in our secret thoughts, we charge Him with neglect and indifference. However, the truth is that His care is infinitely superior to any possibilities of human care, and He, who counts the very hairs on our heads and will not let one sparrow fall to the ground without His awareness, takes note of the minutest matters that can affect the lives of His children and regulates them all according to His own perfect will.

God is our Father and He loves us, and He knows just what is best for us. Therefore, His will is the most perfect thing for us under any circumstance. This can, of course, be difficult to understand. It really would seem as if God's own children were more afraid of His will than of anything else in life, yet His good, pleasing, and perfect will brings only lovingkindness, tender mercy, deep joy, and peace. These are all things God has promised in His Word. When I agree that the will of God for me is good—this can be a difficult thing to do—and when I know He has my best interests in view, I can say, "Yes, Lord, Your will be done."

We are constantly praying one of two things (sometimes in words, sometimes in thoughts, but always in actions): *Lord, help me do what pleases You,* or *Lord, let me do what pleases me.* If we are honest with God, He will show us which of these two prayers we often use. Some of us use the first prayer in the morning and the second prayer throughout the day. The second is inevitably our true desire. Some people vary between the two, which leads to up-and-down lives. Some prayers grow more and more into the first as an all-day prayer, and our lives grow stronger and steadier, more dependable, and much more peaceful.

AM I LIVING WITHIN THE CIRCLE?

We need to ask ourselves, am I living within the circle of God's will for me? Here we are referring to a deeper relationship than merely claiming Christ as Savior and going our own way. Rather, am I committed to going His way, to walking in obedience to His will—not wanting to go counter to His will but to cooperate with Him? Have I made that basic life choice to seek His will and way above my own?

It's important to remember that yielding to God's will does not assure us an easy life or that we will get all we think we should have, but in the face of a heartache, yielding is the first step to peace. We must ask if our will is aligned with God's will. Sometimes we may experience a stubborn, inward resistance and a clinging to our own way that we may not want to recognize, but according to Jeremiah 17:9, "The human heart is the most deceitful of all things, and desperately wicked." It is good to ask the Holy Spirit for His gentle work of instruction and illumination. Jeremiah 17:10 further explains that the Lord searches "all hearts and examine[s] secret motives."

If we are to believe that God does know what is best for us and if we are going to be able to follow His will, we need to have a growing understanding and trust of His promises to us.

What, then, are God's promises?

MAKE IT PERSONAL

1. What negative ideas have you or some of your friends had about the will of God?

2. Write out the promise of Jeremiah 29:11, personalizing it for yourself (e.g., changing "you" to "me"). If this verse is true, how might it apply to your current circumstances?

3. Each morning this week, ask God to help you check out which prayer you are consciously or unconsciously praying during the day:

   Let me do what pleases me, or Help me do what pleases you. At the end of the day, think through your attitudes and actions, and pray for God to reveal your habit of life in this respect.

CHAPTER 2

God's Incredible Promise

For twenty years, Dr. Helen Roseveare served as a medical missionary in Zaire. During the 1964 Simba rebellion, she watched with sorrow as several of her coworkers were cruelly beaten and brutally murdered. She herself was stomped on by the guerilla soldiers until her nose, jaw, and several ribs were broken. Then she was moved from one prison camp to another, never knowing what would happen the next day. Rape was also common.

"I had, in advance," Helen wrote, "geared myself to accept that God had the right to require anything of me that fit into His purpose. God was the Lord of my life, and I trusted Him completely. [During that time] I learned that God is always present tense. . . . When He says 'My grace is sufficient,' He means it. It's not, 'My grace will be sufficient for tomorrow's problems'; it is, 'My grace is sufficient for your immediate, present-tense needs.'"[1]

Helen Roseveare was fully committed to the will of God and knew what it meant to claim the promise of 2 Corinthians 12:9 in her present situation. If we are people committed to going God's way, living inside the circle of His will, then we, too, will experience the comfort and strength that comes from claiming the promises He has given His children in His Word. We will be able to take a promise such as Romans 8:28, claim it, and confidently trust that God will make it true in our present set of circumstances.

"And we know that God causes everything to work together for the good of those who love God and are called according to His purpose" (Rom. 8:28).

Reading this verse carefully, I realize God is telling me He is making this incredible promise true in the particular events of my life, today and every day. God is orchestrating all the activities, people, and situations that will influence my life. He will see to it that all these conditions will work together for good. For whose good—God's or ours? Both. And because of what we know of God's goodness and love for us (see chapter 8), we can be sure it will work for our good. And because we know that God will not give His glory to another, we can be sure it will also work for His good and for His glory.

AN UNCONDITIONAL PROMISE

Earlier in Romans, we were told that those who love God are those who have His Spirit, and verse 16 tells us that if we have His Spirit, we are God's children. If we are His children, we are also His heirs (v. 17). God cannot break His promises to His own children; therefore, the promise of Romans 8:28 is an unconditional promise. Once we have become children of God and have His Spirit within us, no matter what we do—through the sinful choices we make or the rejection of God's will for our lives—the promise of Romans 8:28 still applies to us. He *will* work everything for our good.

What is conditional is our experience of His promise. If we are not within the circle of God's will, although the promise still applies, we cannot experience the comfort, peace, hope, or strength of this promise.

For example, if we choose to have an extramarital affair, even in our sin God is *still* working for our good. As our lives becomes increasingly messy and difficult, and as we experience the damage and hurt of our sinful choices and see the damage and hurt we have caused others, we cannot truly experience the benefits of trusting the promise in Romans 8:28 until we have repented and come back to the circle of God's will for our lives.

This is not to say that people who are not within God's will can never experience anything good from God. However, it is because of His mercy and grace that reaches out to everyone that we can accomplish His own larger purposes, and God often brings blessings to His children who are not walking in His way, as well as to those who are not His children. This blessing to God's wayward children and those who are not His children is found in Romans 2:4: "His kindness is intended to turn you from your sin," where "He gives his sunlight to both the evil and the good, and he sends rain on the just and the unjust alike," as it says in Matthew 5:45.

WORKING FOR OUR GOOD?

Romans 8:28 doesn't promise that all circumstances are good, and it doesn't mean God is working to make us happy or give us what we want in a specific situation, nor does it say that God causes all things to happen. (More on this in chapter 9.) Many things may come to us from the evil motives and intentions of others, but God is big enough and His promise is good enough to see to it that, in the end, circumstances will work together for our good as we yield to Him and trust Him. Even if we rebel against God, He continues to pursue us. He promises to use every circumstance, even those that are a result of our sinful choices, for our ultimate good. What a faithful God we have! Romans 8:31 says, "What shall we say about such wonderful things as these? If God is for us, who can ever be against us?"

Therefore, if the good He is working is not simply the promise of an easy life or to give us what we want, what is this "good"?

God's desire is to conform us to be like His Son. Romans 8:29 says, "For God knew His people in advance, and He chose them to become like His Son." God knows the best thing for us as we live in this broken world is that we become increasingly like Jesus. He also knows that we will be more effective in fulfilling His greater and larger purposes if our characters are more Christlike. He will even take the evilest thing that happens to us and use it to fulfill His purposes in the lives of others. This is the good that He promises to work in our lives.

But in many cases it will be months or even years after the distressing event, the difficulty, the heartache, or the rejection before we will see God's promises unfold, as described in the life of Dr. Helen Roseveare.[2]

In a radio interview, Dr. Helen Roseveare was asked, "Have you seen any good come from your horrible experience of being raped and beaten?"

"Yes," she recalled. "I have seen good come in a number of ways, but one has been especially meaningful."

After speaking at a college, she noticed two girls lingering near the front. "The older of the two came up to me. 'Could you please speak with my sister? Five weeks ago she was raped and has not spoken one word since.'

In the space of a few brief moments, the girl threw her arms around me and broke into heartrending sobs. For the next two hours we wept and shared together as she poured out all her feelings and hurts."

She said, "Later that night as I went to bed, reflecting back on the dreadful experiences I went through during those dark nights deep in the Congo many years earlier, I could see how God does bring good from evil." [3]

We may never see how God has worked life together for good until we see Him face-to-face. Then all life's mysteries will be made plain and we will see how His love and power worked good for us in that situation that seemed disastrous at the time. For now, we may need to be content with the promise, even though we do not know the final outcome.

We may not always understand, but we can always trust in what He has promised.

MAKE IT PERSONAL

1. Who can claim the promise of Romans 8:28?
2. Why might we not feel the benefit of this promise?
3. Read Romans 8:28 from several versions.

Choose the one that makes it clearest for you, write it out, and memorize it. Make a list of all the "things" that are happening in your life right now. How might trusting in the promise of Romans 8:28 impact your view of these circumstances?

CHAPTER 3

Is Everything under God's Control?

But what about those who have not chosen to go God's way, those who live outside the circle of His will? Not everyone is interested in going God's way. Some people are more interested in going their own way and focusing on what pleases themselves. Others may act out of greed or jealousy, and we may be the victims of their actions. How do I deal with the consequences of others' choices and lifestyles which may cause me hurt and pain?

In our diagram, let's place an X outside the circle of God's will to represent that person who is not interested in cooperating with God.

GOD'S WILL

Experiencing the
benefit of
Romans 8:28

These people do not desire to walk in line with His purposes. They are not willing to bring their wills into agreement with God's will. They may try to control us and others in their lives—either openly or with cunning—so that we will do as they desire. And sometimes that brings great pain to us. Amy shares an illustration that fits this point well.

Amy's Story: *I still remember the feeling of total rejection the night my Dad threw us out of our family home. Over a period of years we had watched our dad move further and further away from the faith he had once passionately professed, abandoning the vows he had made before God—to love and cherish his wife and family. We were victims of these choices, and the consequences were emotional and physical abuse, and finally—total abandonment.*

Growing up in this environment, I had experienced, not just physical pain, but also the pain of rejection, shame, loneliness, and powerlessness. And now here we were, unsure of what the future would hold. The questions and doubts about God and His character came flooding in. Could He really be trusted? Had He really seen my pain? Did He really care?

Watching my mother as she made difficult choices and took great steps of faith was one of the most influential things in my life at this time. She taught me much about what it means to trust in a loving God who is in control, even when we suffer at the hands of others. I now know with absolute clarity that God had a bigger plan in mind for my life, a plan that would make use of all that pain.

As my relationship with God grew, I discovered a good, just, and powerful God who had always been there and who had always seen me. He had seen my father's ill treatment of me and of all of us. He had seen me when I had lain awake frightened by what was going on in the next room. He had seen the ways in which my father had manipulated and alienated me from good friends. He had seen the confused and hurting teenager I would become. He had seen the wounds I would carry into my adult relationships.

Though there were many negative consequences as a result of these early experiences, I can see clearly how God has used them to help me become an empathic and compassionate person, someone who can be trusted with the secrets, pain, and shame of others. Looking back, I can see how all of these experiences have equipped me to be of help to others as I have counseled them and helped them to trust in God's loving control.

THE CIRCLE OF GOD'S CONTROL

Is God limited by the wrong choices people around us make? Can He do anything with or to that person who is not walking in His ways? Yes, God is God—all knowing, all powerful, all wise. He reigns over the world of people and events. Even though a person may not embrace His will, no one can escape being within the sphere of His overall control.[1]

The bigger circle now includes both the person who has chosen to go God's way and the person who is not interested in cooperating with God's purposes, and who might even make life difficult for the one who is. We will call this outer circle the circle of God's control.

The words "God's control" are used in the sense that God is bigger than any person or situation that affects our lives, and not in the sense that God merely uses people as little puppets and pulls a few strings to control them. He does not manipulate us. He does not force or coerce people to operate in a certain way against their choices. No, He has given us a will and the power to choose. Therefore, sometimes we find ourselves subjects of the evil choices and actions of others, or recipients of unwanted and even devastating circumstances.

In the Old Testament (Genesis 37 and 39–41), we read about a man called Joseph who had eleven brothers. Joseph was his father's favorite, and his brothers were very jealous of the gifts and special treatment Joseph received. Eventually they orchestrated a plan in which he was sold into slavery to some traders heading for Egypt. In time, Joseph ended up the second most powerful man in all of Egypt, and when a famine struck, he saved his family. The family of Joseph were the ancestors of the children of Israel, and ultimately became the nation into which Jesus was born.

Joseph's brothers are an excellent example of people operating outside of God's will. God did not put hate in their hearts for Joseph—the brothers chose to hate him. However, God's purposes for Joseph (and ultimately His whole-world purpose through the situation) were far higher than the pain and sorrow Joseph experienced temporarily because of his brothers' choice to go the way of hate. In the end, Joseph, his whole family, and his entire nation were saved. In this sense, God was the overall orchestrator of events.[2]

Joseph found rest and comfort in the fact that One bigger than himself, bigger than all the people who misunderstood him, mistreated him, rejected him, lied about him, and forgot their promises to him, was in control and could be trusted. In each valley experience in Joseph's life, he responded to the adversity with acceptance and trust so that others realized God was with him. As he calmly trusted, God caused him to be successful and honored by those in charge so that he was given responsibility and authority wherever he was—in prison or in the palace.

When Joseph's brothers recognized him as the one to whom they had been so cruel, Joseph didn't take vengeance by denying them grain, nor did he take this opportunity to shame them or get even with them for the evil they had done to him earlier. Rather, he spoke kindly to comfort them, recognizing God's hand in it all.

"But don't be upset, and don't be angry with yourselves for selling me to this place. It was God who sent me here ahead of you to preserve your lives . . . It was God who sent me here, not you! And he is the one who made me an adviser to Pharaoh—the manager of his entire palace and the governor of all Egypt." And again, "You intended to harm me, but God intended it all for good." (Gen. 45:5, 8; 50:20).

Though his brothers had acted out of jealousy and hate, Joseph looked beyond the wickedness they had intentionally done to him and acknowledged God was using it to accomplish His purposes. He gave God credit for all the good things that happened to him and trusted God in the adversities, whether they came through people with good or evil intentions.

In Ecclesiastes, Solomon refers to the ups and downs of life as times of prosperity and times of adversity—easy times and hard times, happy times and heavy times. We all know both kinds of experiences. That is what life is like. Heaven will be different, but for now we each will have our share of times of adversity and times of prosperity. Solomon says, "Realize that both come from God" (Eccles. 7:14).

There will be times in your life marked by peace and quiet, joy and laughter, when the road is easy and smooth. There will also be times when life is heavy, the road is rough, and the way is difficult—times of adversity. Jesus told us we should expect this. "Here on this earth you will have many trials and sorrows. But take heart, because I have overcome the world" (John 16:33).

Yes, there will be people in our lives who choose to go their own way, not God's, but that does not bind God's hands. He is still in control of the people who affect our lives. He will work His purposes of good for us in spite of what they do.

But what about Satan? Can God control him?

One of the oldest books of the Bible tells the story of Job. The almost inconceivable events of Job's life all started when Satan came back from looking things over on the earth. From what we know of Satan in other parts of the Bible, we can be quite sure he was up to no good—looking for someone he could accuse or tempt or discourage or deceive.[3]

It is as though God wanted to draw Satan's attention to Job when He said, "Have you noticed my servant Job? He is the finest man in all the earth. He is blameless—a man of complete integrity. He fears God and stays away from evil."

Satan replied to the Lord, "Yes, but Job has good reason to fear God. You have always put a wall of protection around him and his home and his property. You have made him prosper in everything he does. Look how rich he is! But reach out and take away everything he has, and he will surely curse you to your face!"

"All right, you may test him," the Lord said to Satan. "Do whatever you want with everything he possesses, but don't harm him physically." (Job 1:8–12)

Afterward, Job was going along with his regular activities when a servant came to announce a tragedy. While that servant was speaking, a second servant announced a second tragedy. While he was still speaking, a third servant came along and announced a third tragedy. Job's camels, oxen, sheep, donkeys, and servants had been stolen, burned, or wiped away in one way or another. Only a few servants escaped to tell the story. At this time Job was the richest man in all the East. The Bible records that he had over 10,000 animals and "very many servants." Now his riches were wiped out.

But that wasn't all. While that third servant was speaking, a fourth came with the most devastating news: Job's seven sons and three daughters were feasting together in a house when a big wind came along, blew the house down, and all ten children died.[4]

What do you think Job did or said when he received word of this incredible loss? What would you do if just one child or one friend were killed in an accident, or if your life's savings were wiped out? What would you say? The Bible tells us Job worshiped God.[5] In the midst of every crisis, whether big or small, we need to first remember who God is and worship Him. He is so powerful, He can accomplish all that His wisdom, love, and goodness has planned. Therefore, even though we do not understand what has happened to us or why He allowed it, we can worship Him.

THE LORD GAVE—DID SATAN TAKE AWAY?

Job's first words after he silently worshiped God were, "The Lord gave me what I had, and the Lord has taken it away" (Job 1:21). It may seem at first that Satan had taken everything away. He used the Sabeans and the Chaldeans and the fire and the wind to accomplish his dreadful, destructive feat, but God had put a limit on how far Satan could go, and he couldn't go any farther than that.

Job knew God was in charge. He knew something of God's name, something of His character, something of His attributes. Job was confident that God reigned. So, in effect, Job might have said, "Since God is all knowing, all powerful, and in charge, He could have changed things. But God didn't."

Notice Job did not say, "The Lord gave, and the Sabeans, the fire, the Chaldeans, or the wind has taken it all away." He did not even say, "The Lord gave, and Satan has taken it all away." Job looked beyond people and events to the God who sat above all and was in control of all, and he acknowledged that the One who had taken away was the same One who had given in the first place. Therefore, Job chose instead to declare, "The Lord gave me what I had, and the Lord has taken it away." And with these words, Job acknowledged God's control. Even though God was in control of Job's life and He is in control of our lives, how should we respond when Satan seems to be at work through the chaos in our lives? Where does Satan fit into all this?

IS SATAN IN THE CIRCLE?

Where should we place Satan in our diagram? Can God do anything about Satan? Yes, and Satan belongs right inside the circle of God's control.

When the Bible tells us that God is the Almighty One, it means precisely that: He is all mighty. Another verse says, "Because [He] who lives in you is greater than [he] who lives in the world." Who is the "He" who is in you? That person is God, who is also the person of the Holy Spirit who lives within us, and He (God, "who lives in you") is greater than Satan ("he who lives in the world").[6]

Even Satan recognized this biblical truth. In Job 1:10, Satan said, "You have always put a wall of protection around him and his home and his property." Satan would have loved to destroy Job, but he knew he couldn't get through the wall God had put around Job without God's permission. Notice the limited permission God gave to Satan: "Do whatever you want with everything he possesses, but don't harm him physically" (Job 1:12). God opened the wall around Job only so far. Satan could touch all that Job owned, but he could not touch the man himself.

So Satan went out and started his incredibly destructive work. Four tragic events resulted in Job losing all his riches and his ten children. But remember, Satan was limited. At this point he couldn't touch Job himself. When Job still chose to worship God, Satan wasn't ready to give up. "But reach out and take away his health, and he will surely curse you to your face!" Then God chose to give Satan permission to take Job's health, but not his life. Satan once more went out and did what he could, but again he was limited.[7]

God has constructed a wall around us, His people. Nothing good or bad, nor anyone intending good or bad, including Satan, man, or events, can pass through that wall and touch us except as God directs or allows.

This wall is not a special force field that God puts around Christians to make them exempt from troubles. This wall doesn't shield us from the problems and sufferings inherent in this fallen world, but we can be sure that the trouble has been granted permission—passing through the will of our loving Father—before it touches us, regardless of the originating agent.

Psalm 125:2 expresses this same truth in another way: "Just as the mountains surround Jerusalem, so the Lord surrounds his people, both now and forever." Psalm 57:1 describes us taking refuge under the shadow of His wings, and Psalm 18 describes God as our rock, our fortress, and our deliverer. Another significant dimension to our diagram then is this: God has put a wall or mountains about His children.

And it is through this wall that the atmosphere of God's love and protection surrounds us, protecting us from the evil that would seek to harm us.

THE ATMOSPHERE OF GOD'S LOVE

What happened to Job came to him through the atmosphere of God's loving care and protection. God allowed Satan to do some evil and destructive things, but God didn't close His eyes. He was still wide awake, with nothing out of His control or too much for Him to handle. He was filtering it all through His character.

God can never act contrary to Himself—to any of His attributes. He filters all things through

- His love, which is full of compassion,
- His wisdom, which cannot be in error,
- His goodness, which cannot fail, and
- His power, which cannot be restrained.

The ultimate result was for the good of Job, his family and friends, and his "miserable comforters," and for the glory of God.

Job is not the only biblical example that shows how God opens the wall and allows Satan's evil intentions and work to come through. Remember the "thorn in the flesh," that "messenger of Satan" sent to torment Paul? God allowed this to come through Paul's wall of protection, and for good reason—which Paul recognized and accepted—to keep him from being conceited.[8]

Satan is real and mighty, but God is *almighty*. Sometimes God allows Satan to test and try His children because He is in the process of accomplishing a greater purpose. Satan was allowed to test even God's own Son. At other times God is greatly glorified in preventing Satan from interfering in our lives. Although we can rest assured that God is not intimidated by Satan, we are told to personally resist Satan, his attacks, and his temptations. We are assured that Satan's temptations will not be more than we can bear, because God delights in delivering His children from Satan's activity.[9]

Satan is evil and he incites men and women to do evil. Just as God does not cause Satan's evil activities, God does not cause people to do evil things, such as murder, rape, cause rejection, or display envy. But He sometimes allows the evil of Satan or the evil or wrong choices of others to impact His children, and He, of course, knows about it.

However, Satan has never snuck around to do his devastating work, unnoticed by God. If Satan could get around without God noticing, then he would be more powerful than God. If God is not actually overseeing and permitting what happens, how can we trust Him? How can we trust that God has control of our concerns if Satan is allowed to come along and spoil them without any restraints? How can we have faith in a God who is not actually in charge?

Hannah Whitall Smith explains it so clearly:

Second causes must all be under the control of our Father, and not one of them can touch us except with His knowledge and by His permission. It may be the sin of man that originates the action, and therefore the thing itself cannot be said to be the will of God; but by the time it reaches us, it has become God's will for us and must be accepted as directly from His hands. No man or company of men, no power in earth or heaven, can touch that soul which is abiding in Christ without first passing through His encircling presence and receiving the seal of His permission. If God be for us, it matters not who may be against us; nothing can disturb or harm us, except He shall see that it is best for us and shall stand aside to let it pass.[10]

Therefore, in every situation, God is wide awake and in control, and whatever Satan does, either directly through his messengers or through people or events, is Father-filtered—past, present, and future.

ALL OF LIFE IS FATHER-FILTERED

Some of you may be thinking, *That's not my concern. My problem is my past. What about the sins I committed before I became a Christian?*

The good news is, God's control not only embraces the circumstances and people who surround our lives now, but He also embraces the past. Whether pleasant or difficult, life hasn't happened by chance. For example, do you look back on your life and say, "If only I hadn't married the person I married!" Perhaps you made a bad choice out of rebellion or infatuation, or perhaps it was made with both parties seeking God's will, but the marriage hasn't turned out to be what you had hoped for. It may be that your spouse has turned against you or against the Lord or is creating difficulties you hadn't anticipated. However, God begins where you are, right this moment. You must recognize that God permitted the union or circumstance that you are currently in. He didn't cause it. You made the choice, but He permitted it, and perhaps He even permitted your husband or wife to develop undesirable traits. These are a trial to you. God has had and still has control of the people and the situations as they now impact you and your life.

Stewing about the past, fretting in the present, and looking anxiously to the future are all futile when you have a loving heavenly Father who cares for you and is in control of all the people, events, and circumstances that now affect and impact your life.[11]

Whether . . .

you lose your job,

your children misbehave,

it rains and your barbecue plans are ruined,

your spouse becomes an alcoholic,

you discover you can't get pregnant,

you get sick before a trip away,

you lose a close friend to cancer,

or

(fill in your own current situation),

. . . determine to acknowledge everything that happens in the humdrum or the crises of your life is either directed or permitted by our loving Father, who is quite awake and in control. Only our all-wise, all-loving, only-good God knows what is best and what will ultimately contribute to the good of His children growing toward Christlikeness. Our God does reign, and that includes everything and everyone who impacts my life.

Throughout the Old and New Testaments, we see clear evidence that God is in control. He is in charge of all things in the world of nature, nations, people, and events—even Satan. Several verses in Scripture illustrate this:

O Lord, God of our ancestors, you alone are the God who is in heaven. You are ruler over all the kingdoms of the earth. You are powerful and mighty; no one can stand against you! (2 Chron. 20:6)

Praise the Lord! For the Lord our God, the Almighty, reigns. (Rev. 19:6)

God is never unobservant. He neither stands aloof nor does He ever wring His hands, helplessly wondering what to do. He can and does intervene in the affairs of nations and people. When we start to see our life's circumstances as filtered through God Himself, we will experience less of the stresses and anxieties that could otherwise plague us.

So what is God's purpose in allowing these difficult circumstances into our lives?

MAKE IT PERSONAL

1. What is the difference between the person who is only living in the circle of God's control and the person who is also living within the circle of God's will?

2. Copy the circle diagram from page 17. Take your list of circumstances from chapters 1 and 2 and write each one within the circle of God's control.

   Make a list of the key people in your lives, those you care about or those who have an impact on you. Write these people's names within the circle of God's control as well.

   Are there any circumstances or people you struggle to believe are really under God's control? Why is this?

3. When we understand and believe that God is in control, no other truth can offer such peace to the heart. Read Isaiah 40:12–31. How do these verses apply to the circumstances or people you struggle to believe are under God's control?

CHAPTER 4

The Bigger Picture: God's Master Plan

God's master plan is a bit like trying to complete a large jigsaw puzzle consisting of a thousand tiny pieces. There is hardly enough room to spread the pieces on one table. You start by turning all the pieces picture side up, then you begin with the obvious—the corners, the face of a person, or part of a large object. Most of the pieces by themselves have no meaning until they became part of the whole picture. Of course, you do have the advantage of guessing how the puzzle is put together via the finished picture on the box.

But as far as the big picture of our lives is concerned, God is the only One who knows what the finished picture looks like. For now, all we have is His Romans 8:28 promise, "And we know that God causes everything to work together for the good of those who love God and are called according to his purpose." Though we may not see the good in any single piece of the puzzle, as He fits the pieces together over the years, they begin to mold and fit into a pattern meant for good.

God knows where He's going in our lives, and He's taking us the best way to get there. Our present heartaches, financial instability, distressing family problems, and perplexing circumstances are simply pieces He has allowed in the puzzle, and He knows just which shaped pieces to place into our lives next. Because He sees the bigger picture of our entire earthly lives and into eternity, He knows how they fit into the individual circumstances of our lives.

In the book of Ruth, we learn about a woman called Naomi. Before all the pieces of her life were together, Naomi pronounced judgment on God's ways in her life:

Don't call me Naomi [which means pleasant]. . . . instead call me Mara [which means bitter], for the Almighty has made life very bitter for me, I went away full, but the Lord has brought me home empty. Why call me Naomi when the Lord has caused me to suffer and the Almighty has sent such tragedy upon me? (Ruth 1:20–21)

It is true that not everything in Naomi's life was good or pleasant, as we would call it. Naomi's husband and her two sons had died in a foreign land. One of her daughters-in-law had left her, and Naomi had no material possessions. All she could see were the seemingly tragic pieces that didn't make sense.

Later, when the pieces came together, the puzzle became a beautiful picture. Naomi's daughter-in-law, Ruth, was better to Naomi than seven sons would have been. Ruth's future husband, Boaz, not only became their provider, but he became the father of Naomi's grandchildren. And perhaps best of all, Naomi was back in her own land with her own people.

The Bible says that God's ways are perfect. We may not have a sense of this as the pieces are going together, but the pieces have to be considered as part of the whole. We must learn to trust that all His will is good, pleasing, and acceptable as we wait in faith for Him to finalize all the pieces, working them together into the pattern of our lives for good.

Perhaps you can look back to a time when you were perplexed and discouraged because God didn't answer your prayer in the way you wanted or at the time you expected. You may even have entertained the thought that God had forsaken you or didn't care, but now you can see where you might have been if He had answered that prayer as you had wanted Him to.

Our perspective is so narrow, and we look for God to come into our lives in circumstances and events that please us. Therefore we would not put that dark piece of the puzzle in next. "No," we say, "let's work on this bright spot—it's so pleasant and cheery."

Oswald Chambers says we need to give God elbow room, give Him the right to be God in our lives, and "always be in a state of expectancy, and see that you leave room for God to come in as He likes."[1]

We need to be prepared for God to work in unexpected and sometimes unwanted ways. It might be missing the plane. It might be a night of interrupted sleep before a meeting. It might be far more intense trouble or suffering—the desertion of a spouse, the running away of a child, a broken engagement, a terminal illness, the loss of a loved one, or a son with mental illness. Through it all, God is at work in our lives and wants more than anything else to conform us to the image of His Son.

Will shares his story of seeing God work in his own life.

Will's Story: *After I got married, I thought my life was going to be perfect. My wife and I quickly started accumulating all the things that trap a young professional couple: a new house, new furniture, a new car, and plenty of trips abroad on holiday. But before long we ended up in major debt. Despite taking out loans, we continued to overspend. Eventually, we got to the point where we were surviving on short-term, high-interest loans to make it to the end of the month. We had really blown it and felt completely desperate. We were filled with a sense of shame and failure. We were able to get some help to start sorting out our finances, but it was going to be a long, difficult road. How could anything good come out of our irresponsible choices?*

God gives us some surprising promises for times when we feel we have blown it and all is a loss. When we can see no way that this piece of the puzzle is working "together for good," God says, "I will give you back what you lost" and "will reclaim for My glory those years that seem to you to be filled with useless rubble because of your failures" (paraphrase of Joel 2:25). We can know that even the consequences of our own sins and failures are included in the amazing promise that God will cause all things to work together for good.

With God, there is forgiveness and restoration as He allows us to begin again. "He will give a crown of beauty for ashes, a joyous blessing instead of mourning, festive praise instead of despair" (Isa. 61:3). We can depend upon God's superabundant grace to transform our hurts, disappointments, failures, sins—and even our abuses—into benefits. That's grace! That is the transforming grace of our loving, forgiving, restoring Lord. He promises to transform the ashes into something beautiful and useful.

Will's story continues:

With God's help and with support from our church community, we are finally being better managers of the finances God has given us. But the amazing thing is, God has used our financial failures for good. Because we lived on a very tight budget for many years, people who didn't have much money felt comfortable in our home and accepted by us. By His grace, God has transformed what seemed only a loss and turned it to something that could help others as they struggled with these same issues.

In addition to these promises applying to sins we commit ourselves, they also apply to sins committed by others against us. So many wounded and hurting among us need to know that these same promises apply to those who have experienced all kinds of abuse. Some have had excruciatingly painful wounds inflicted upon them by the sins of others over which they had no control. Elaine grew up with only boys for playmates, but she was in her element, climbing trees and building treehouses. She shares her story:

Elaine's Story: *Our favorite project was building dens. It was there that it happened—the thing that was to haunt me for years. In one of our dens, where no adults would ever see, I was raped by a young boy while the others watched! From then on, I lived under the shadow of their threat, "Don't ever tell or we'll beat you up." And I knew they would. One of the rippling effects of that rape in the den was that whenever they "wanted me," I had to be at their disposal. It got to the point that I believed this was what men were for, and women were just "there for them." It gave me such a wrong view of men, even though I was so young. I couldn't share this with anyone, and I lived with a constant sense of guilt and overwhelming fear. I hated those boys and transferred that "hate" to my parents. My inner cry to them was, Why don't you ever ask me why I'm so unhappy or why I'm afraid to play with those boys? Or to God, Why don't You zap them with a piece of lightning or make this den fall down on them as punishment for this terrible hurt they caused me? As I began to mature in body, I knew it was wrong. I knew God wouldn't be pleased, but I couldn't deal with that either. It was a nightmare through my teen years. Many years later I was able to talk to someone and get help.*

But God! Yes, God is able to bring beauty out of the ashes of an unfortunate past. I have a deeper understanding of anyone who has been abused this way. I feel their pain, and my heart longs to help them bring it to the surface and deal with it. For a number of years I worked at summer camps. The young girls entrusted to me were often filled with hurts like I had lived with. Because of my experience, I was able to be sensitive to their problems, and in a caring and loving way help them to open up about it. When I would say, "I know a bit of how you feel because a similar thing happened to me," their mouths would drop open as they exclaimed, "What a relief! Finally it's been told! And someone understands!" Later God also gave me an opportunity to counsel young women over the phone while volunteering at our local crisis pregnancy center.

Elaine's experience is one more example that shows God's transforming power by His overruling grace in our lives. He can redeem bad situations, turning them into ministry opportunities in ways that are "far more than we would ever dare to ask or even dream of—infinitely beyond our highest prayers, desires, thoughts, or hopes."[2]

Scores of people have written books or shared through interviews how God took a devastating experience, such as sexual abuse, a shattered marriage, financial collapse, or the wounds from growing up in a dysfunctional family, and turned it into something beautiful for personal growth or for useful ministry.

It is essential that we believe God is in everything, because it is the very foundation for our faith. If, as a believer, God is not in sovereign control of your life—even when you disobey Him—then you will have a limited expectation of when and under what circumstances you can expect God to be involved. You must believe that even when you have disobeyed Him, God will use that for your ultimate good, consequences and all.

These are the facts, and you've no doubt already discovered that by simply knowing God is in control, He has a master plan in mind that does not necessarily spell "heart" peace. There's still a piece of the puzzle missing.

Why do you need God's grace right now? For the small frustration of an interruption? The confusion of why things are going "differently"? Or is it to cover a more crucial matter—sickness, pain, sorrow? We encourage you to affirm His grace even though your feelings speak a contrary message: "I can't understand." Let's add to that, "but I can trust."

God wants to conform us to the image of His Son, using us to minister grace to others, giving us strength for the journey, and sharing with others His stored-up goodness along the way. And all those tiny pieces fit into the larger goal: His finished picture.

MAKE IT PERSONAL

1. What do we mean when we say God has the bigger picture in mind? What is He moving toward in our lives?

2. Beyond our small world, God's bigger picture also includes how we fit into His great world plan and purpose. What are some of the things this includes, and how do they relate to you? See Matthew 28:18–20, 2 Corinthians 5:18–20, and 1 Peter 2:4–5.

3. Give some illustrations—either out of your own life or the lives of others—as to how God brought forth beauty out of what you or they felt were the ashes of past sins and mistakes.

CHAPTER 5

Being Sure of God's Loving Control

In any and every situation, we can know in our minds that God is in control. We can even believe He has filtered all things that come to us or He could have changed things. But we can still choose to shake our fist in His face with clenched teeth and fiery eyes and say, "God, I don't like what You've done or what You've allowed into my life." However, John's experience shows the opposite.

John's Story: *I was in the doctor's office, and the doctor hastily entered the small room, quickly scanned the notes given to him by the nurse, and said, "John, you have cancer."*

This was not the result I had been expecting. My father had similar problems at my age and also had an enlarged prostate. I had considered the remote possibility of prostate cancer and had discussed it with my wife, but I suppose I had mentally dismissed it as a possibility.

"The good news is that only two of the eight samples showed cancer," he went on. Then he spent the next fifteen minutes going through some possible treatment plans as I sat in a sort of dreamlike state, taking in the implications of what he had just said. "Go home and talk to your wife," the doctor said, "and I will see you in about four weeks to discuss what we are going to do about it."

I phoned my wife as soon as I left the room and shared my state of shock with her. I remember thinking on the way home that there was a real possibility I could be in heaven a lot sooner than I had previously anticipated.

In coming to terms with this news over the next few days and weeks, I gained a new perspective on some issues as I talked to my wife, and perhaps more significantly, as I talked honestly to God. Among other things, I thought quite a lot about heaven. What will it be like? What does it mean to be eternal? Some of the songs I listened to took on a different significance.

"You give and take away."

"Even though I walk through the valley of death—still I will praise You."

Being "forced" to face up to the possibility of dying led me to question in a way I had never had to before the truth of verses such as Romans 8:28: "And we know that God causes everything to work together for the good of those who love God and are called according to his purpose for them." I very quickly came to understand that nothing in this life could compare with what it would be like to actually be with Christ, to have my redemption completed, to receive the "well done, good and faithful servant," and to share in Christ's glory! Going home to heaven was the best thing that could happen. It was the ultimate good thing.

Thanks to a lot of very skilled medics and the prayers of many close friends, I received the all-clear result about four months later. But looking back on those months of uncertainty, I have to say I learned a lot through that experience. My perspective has changed on what is important in life.

Most of the time, the piece of the puzzle that's missing is my response. My response in difficult circumstances is incredibly significant because it determines whether or not I find comfort in the truth that God is in control and that He reigns in the circumstances that affect me, His child. My response determines whether I am overwhelmed with frustration, stress, pressure, unmanageable pain, resentment, and bitterness, or whether I choose to experience the peace that surpasses understanding.[1]

JOB'S WORDS REVEAL HIS RESPONSE

We see the importance of the right response in the story of Job. After all those tragedies happened to him in just a brief span of time, we see that he first worshiped God. Only after he worshiped did he speak. He spoke truth as his mind reviewed the facts. "The Lord gave me what I had, and the Lord has taken it away." But his next words revealed his heart attitude as he added, "Praise the name of the Lord!" (Job 1:21). (Older translations of the Bible use the word *blessed* instead of *praise*.)

In choosing to praise God, Job expressed his heart of trustful submission to God in the face of these disasters. His focus was on the Lord instead of on the tragedies. His major focus wasn't even on the hand of God that allowed the situation, but on the "name of the Lord," the nature of God—that is, who God really is, His character, His attributes. Job chose to believe in God's wisdom, goodness, and love, as well as in His power.

Job chose to praise God in spite of circumstances that seemed to contradict His character. He made a deliberate choice to trust God and praise Him instead of blaming God or accusing Him. Job could have cursed the name of the Lord. He could have charged God with acting unwisely or in an unloving way, or of being inattentive or unfair (arbitrary). Instead of choosing to believe those lies, he proclaimed, "Praise the name of the Lord!" God's Word verifies Job's attitude. It's recorded, "In all of this, Job did not sin by blaming God" (Job 1:22). Job chose to trust God even though he couldn't understand what was happening. This led to Job's acceptance of the situation.

MY RESPONSE TO GOD'S LOVING CONTROL

Notice that Job didn't thank God for the tragedies, but he accepted them. Paul writes in 1 Thessalonians 5:18, "Be thankful in all circumstances." We are not expected to be thankful for the tragedies that occur in our lives, but like Job, we can look to God beyond what is happening and praise Him for His character. Instead of shaking a clenched fist in God's face, Job's attitude was, "Even in this, I can be thankful that my God loves me and promises good to me. I do not understand, but I choose to trust Him."

To be faced with news no one wants to hear provides us an opportunity to respond with great trust in God. In the face of possible loss, grief, and pain, we always have a choice. We can choose to listen to Satan's temptation to curse God for being unfair, unwise, unloving, unkind, inattentive, uncaring, or unable to do anything about it, or we can be like Job and choose to praise God for who He is, trusting that He is in charge of all the conditions of our lives, that He loves us and is working for our best interests. However, our direct, trusting response may be a process.

Our response isn't always easy. Sometimes it's a process, and often there's a struggle involved. To illustrate this, James shares with us his own personal struggle to trust God in hard situations.

James's Story: *Six months ago I was forced to resign from my job position because of deceit, lies, and false promises of some members of the board of directors who wanted their friend placed into my job. I had dedicated myself to this job for many years, and I was so resentful I could not sleep at night, thinking of the men who stood to gain by telling these lies. The bitterness haunted me and affected my family. It encompassed my entire life and conversations to the point that I had no ministry.*
I wanted those men to fall on their faces. I longed for God to teach them a lesson! But life went on for them quite smoothly. I gloated over any bit of information that hinted that they might be having struggles.

I now have a new job that I love in a new town—a place where we had dreamed about living. What more could I want? I should be writing these people thank-you notes for acting deceitfully, but I am still thinking about how I can hurt them back.

It's taken time, but I now realize I need to forgive these men. It has become so clear to me that even in these bad things, God has been fitting and will continue to fit everything into a pattern for good for our family as we respond in a right manner toward the events and the people involved.

Whether immediate or recognized over time, this acknowledgment that God is in complete control of every facet of our lives is essential for our hearts to surrender and confidently trust Him.

INWARD REACTION TO EXTERNAL EVENTS

Through all the varied conditions of our lives planned or permitted by our loving Father, God's one great purpose is to, hour by hour, moment by moment, conform us to the image of Christ. God wants to complete the good work He began in us at salvation. Through the apostle Paul, God promises, "And I am certain that God, who began the good work within you, will continue his work until it is finally finished on the day when Christ Jesus returns" (Phil. 1:6). Far more important to Him than giving us easy lives is the development of our character and our growth in grace. Every person and event entering our lives move us toward that one all-consuming passion of God's heart, that we would be like His Son.[2]

The dynamics of that process is something like this: Nothing anyone does can prevent God's good work in our lives unless we allow it to cause a wrong reaction in our own spirits. It is in this context that growth in grace takes place. It is not what happens to us in life that is most critical, but it is our inward reaction to that external occurrence that fosters either peace or unrest within us.

Although the dynamics contributing to our response may be simple, such as being irritated at the neighbor's dog barking all night when we hoped for a good night's sleep, we can react with irritation and impatience—which only adds more harm to our bodies and souls—or we can respond with acceptance, knowing God allowed this certain situation to happen. This is not to say that acceptance means ignoring the problem if it continues, but the important thing is to make God our first reference and accept the situation.

We may not be able to control what other people do to us or the circumstances that arise, but by God's grace, we can control our response. By His grace, even the most difficult of circumstances do not need to define us for the rest of our lives, nor do we have to remain irreversibly damaged by the actions of others. Instead, as we respond to God with acceptance—confidently trusting, even being thankful in the midst of our circumstances—He will cause all things to work together for our good.

Jesus gave us the same challenge: "I have told you all this so that you may have peace in me. Here on earth you will have many trials and sorrows. But take heart, because I have overcome the world" (John 16:33). Jesus has already overcome. Our part is again explained in those two little words in the middle of that verse, "take heart." Does that mean we have to be happy about the difficult circumstance we are in or put on a brave face for those around us? No. Rather, we are saying in our innermost being, "Lord, I know that You know what You're doing. I believe You are still in control of everything in my life, and I trust You." When we make the choice to trust God like this, we are experiencing what Paul says in Philippians 4:7, "God's peace, which exceeds anything we can understand." Even Paul had to trust God through his own physical conflict, his thorn in the flesh.

PAUL'S THORN: A DIVINE GIFT

A good example of a positive response to God through suffering is Paul's thorn in the flesh (2 Cor. 12:7). J. Oswald Sanders explains it this way:

From his own costly experience, Paul affirmed that his thorn was a Divine gift. "There was given to me a thorn," Paul says, and the thought behind the word "thorn" is "given as a favor"! True, Satan had a part in his testing, for Paul describes it as a messenger of Satan sent to buffet him (v. 7). It was not God who instigated the test, but apparently, as in Job's case, God permitted Satan to sift His servant Paul, and by the time the testing thorn reached him, the thorn had become not "a messenger of Satan," but a gift of God's grace. The thorn in the flesh was given to Paul and not imposed upon him. What appeared to be the expression of Satan's malice proved to be the beneficent gift of God, with a view to Paul's wider ministry. God's love is long-sighted. To Him, the spiritual welfare and growth of His children is of far greater importance than their physical comfort; hence the ministry of suffering. He does not always spare present pain if it will produce eternal profit.

Like Paul, we have the choice to restfully accept our trials as Father-filtered or to become cynical and bitter and let the resentment eat away at our spirits. Sometimes working through our anger takes time before we come to a place of acceptance. Yet if we blame God, blame others, or blame fate, our lives will only end in a lack of peace and misery, wasted so far as our usefulness to God's purposes in the world is concerned.

It is helpful to make a declaration of your faith as a response to God in any situation where you find yourself struggling with resentment, doubt, or confusion. We may pray something like this:

Lord, I accept this situation in faith rather than in resentment and unbelief. I know You know what You're doing, and whatever You allow to enter my life is Father-filtered and comes to me out of Your heart of love. I count this as another event in the "everything" that You will work together for my good.

If we continually bring our feelings of unbelief before the Lord in prayer, being able to see God in everything that happens to us will develop into a life habit. Such a habit is something that must be learned, so that in the midst of any event, little or big, in which we feel our world falling apart, our first thought is of God, our loving Father. Whether we acknowledge Him or not makes all the difference in the world. Such was the case for Thomas.

Thomas's Story: *When my son Jack took suddenly ill with a chest infection and gradually became sicker after a few days of being in the hospital, it became apparent that this was a serious illness and possibly a life-threatening situation.*

Far from making me doubt God's control of this time, this situation actually reaffirmed my faith. It made me realize that my faith—based on the hope of the resurrection—was stronger than I had thought.

I particularly felt the truth from the words of 2 Corinthians 4:8–9, that although I felt hard pressed, perplexed, and struck down by what was happening, I did not feel despair, abandoned, or destroyed.

These feelings were all girded up by the loving, practical, and spiritual support from my church community. Upon reflection after the event, when Jack had made a full recovery, this light and momentary trouble had given me a greater sense of the hope we have in Christ.

No matter what situation we find ourselves in, God is omniscient and knows what is happening to us every moment of every day. He is the One who makes the final decision as to what can and cannot happen to us.

By learning to appropriate these truths in the everyday minor crises, we are building a habit of walking in these truths, mentally bringing God into the situation, and making Him our first reference, then viewing that incident or situation with the thought, *My Father knows all about this.* As the habit is developed and practiced, it will become a lifestyle—a natural response when adversities arise. We will then be able to say, "My Father is in control, and He loves me. I will never think of anything He will forget. Why should I worry? I will trust Him."

This perspective is essential to experiencing a life of peace and joy. Knowing that our God is in control of everything and is there, in charge, doing His work and fulfilling His promises, releases us from resentments that disturb our peace.

MAKE IT PERSONAL

1. Explain the difference between responding to God with a clenched fist or an open hand.

2. Read Psalm 119:65–72, 89–93. How did the Psalmist look upon his trials (afflictions)? Where did he acknowledge they came from, and what did he see them doing for him?

3. What does it mean to make God your first reference? List some everyday events in which you can make God your first reference.

4. This faith declaration was given in the chapter above: Lord, I accept this situation in faith rather than in resentment and unbelief. I know You know what You're doing, and whatever You allow to enter my life is Father-filtered and comes to me out of Your heart of love. I count this as another event in the "everything" that You will work together for my good. (You may also replace the words "this situation" with the specific area of life that is overwhelming you right now. Let this declaration be your response to your loving Father this week as it relates to your specific situation.)

CHAPTER 6

Does Trusting God End All Our Struggles?

If we believe that God is in control and that this is a quick fix to end every struggle and mend every hurt, does this mean there is no need for more information, more challenge, or more encouragement? The truth is that there is no one action we can take and no one truth we can put into practice that will put us on such a high, spiritual plane where we will no longer experience the harsh reality of a deeply fallen people living in a deeply fallen world.

Still, we long to find something to relieve and free us from the continual worries and hurts of life. Many people turn to popular Christian books or teachers who offer quick-fix methods for how to find freedom and happiness. Others may adapt to our culture's way of dealing with difficulties, such as numbing or distracting ourselves with entertainment and consumerism. Many others give up believing the Bible's promise that we can live lives of peace and joy despite our circumstances. However, even if we follow the right path by devoting ourselves more fully to God, we will still experience inner struggle and pain because the overall reality is that we were made for eternity and heaven.

WE WERE MADE FOR HEAVEN

When God created the world, He designed humans for a perfect environment, but that isn't where we are now. We must live for a time in a fallen, sin-infested world composed of an imperfect environment, imperfect people, and imperfect relationships.

We know that in heaven there will be no more death, no more pain, no more sorrow, and no more tears, but we aren't there yet. Jesus said, "Here on earth you will have many trials and sorrows" (John 16:33). From the moment Adam and Eve chose to follow their own will rather than God's, people have suffered troubles, trials, sorrows, and difficulties.

Romans 8:18–28 describes how all of creation groans as if in the pains of childbirth, waiting for the day to be free from death and decay. Just like a woman in childbirth expects the painful process to result in reward for her labor, so we should expect to experience pain and suffering in this life to prepare us for a life of serving God as we await our eternal reward. All the pain in this life prepares us for the greater purpose God has for us.

PAIN HAS A PURPOSE

Developing a realistic view of pain and suffering, and understanding the benefits, helps us better face our inner struggles. Philip Yancey, in *Where Is God When It Hurts?*, points out that physical pain is a good gift from God for the protection and care of the body. Pain also serves as a warning signal that something is wrong and needs attention. Sometimes emotional pain alerts us to wrong thinking or behavior, and as such, emotional pain can also serve to promote the health of our souls. For example, the pain of loneliness may be God's way of letting us know it's time to reach out to someone else. Frustration on our part may be God's way of getting our attention, making us aware that there's something we can do to change our circumstances.

If we feel guilty, it might be that our conscience is prompting us to consider some sin in our lives that needs confessing and repenting, or it could mean something needs correcting in our thinking because we have forgotten we stand before God, forgiven and perfect in His sight (Rom. 5:1).

There are, however, other kinds of pain. A loved one may die and we grieve. A friend may turn against us and we hurt. We may have been raised by alcoholic parents. We may have been abused as children. But inevitably, we will continue to experience emotional and physical pain, suffering, and struggles as long as we are on this earth.

RECONCILED TO THE REALITY OF PAIN

Pain will be with us during our earthly journey. Instead of resisting pain with resentment, we can embrace it with hope, as James 1:2–4 says:

When troubles of any kind come your way, consider it an opportunity for great joy. For you know that when your faith is tested, your endurance has a chance to grow. So let it grow, for when your endurance is fully developed, you will be perfect and complete, needing nothing.

Embracing our pain does not eradicate life's struggles, but it can give us a new perspective as we face them. Instead of enduring a trial full of self-pity or feeling guilty or fighting with a resistant attitude, we can know with confidence that God will use the pain for good in our present lives. It is possible that we may experience full healing in this life, but we always have the certainty that we will be fully delivered from all our pain in heaven. We can let the pain draw us closer to Jesus, allowing us a richer experience of Him. Even though our emotions are giving us contrary messages, we can cry out, "Oh, how great are God's riches and wisdom and knowledge! How impossible it is for us to understand his decisions and his ways!" (Rom. 11:33). We can choose to trust Him even though we don't fully understand His ways at the moment.

Conversely, the pain and struggles of life take on different forms with different people. Diverse personalities and temperaments will experience different struggles and varying degrees of internal suffering. Some people may struggle with questions about truth and doubts about God, while others would not.

Pain also comes because of one's own mistakes and sins. We may need to appropriately work through the grief, the unforgiveness, or the self-understanding. Or sometimes it might mean deeply humbling ourselves to do all we can to mend a relationship. Yet many times even these proper actions will not eradicate the pain. A residual pain lingers.

Pain is also brought on by the loss of respect expressed through belittling, insulting, ignoring, and abusing. Deep pain can come as a result of the death of or the clear rejection from a friend or spouse of many years. Pain comes from many different sources, and though the experiences may have drawn us closer to the Lord and taught us many valuable lessons, there is still the ache in our hearts because of the hurt and the tremendous sense of loss. Even memories of the good times together bring pain and struggle, and sometimes even bring back some of our unanswered questions. The deep hurt and sense of intense pain is always there and will not go away.

To feel pain doesn't mean we are not trusting God adequately. Feeling that pain isn't wrong or unspiritual, but of course, if we allow these feelings to lead us into resentment, anxiety, or even self-accusation, then it is wrong and needs to be confessed and properly dealt with. Hurt, pain, and struggle are all part of the human condition, an inevitable part of living in this imperfect world. Though God does not promise to wipe out the pain, Jesus assures us He will give us the strength to endure it. The struggle may continue, and it may take a long time to experience the good that comes out of suffering, but we can have hope and peace in the midst of it.

In dealing with pain, it is helpful to discern what is the real cause of our struggle. Is it a result of the inevitable pain we feel as a part of a fallen world? Or is it due to a failure to trust God because we don't really know who He is and how He feels toward us?

MAKE IT PERSONAL

1. What are some things we may expect as we live in an imperfect world? Think this through on your own, then with the verses here. Remember, we are not left alone with our struggles now. There is help and hope through Jesus Christ and His written Word. What does He promise us in times of:

   - loss of respect (belittled, insulted, ignored, rejected, etc.)? Psalm 9:9–10,
   - personal weakness and inadequacy? 2 Peter 1:2–4
   - material needs? Matthew 6:31–33
   - grief? Psalm 34:18
   - physical weakness? Psalm 41:1–3
   - growing older? Isaiah 46:4

2. Is there a lingering pain or hurt in your life right now? Are there any verses above that can help you? What other verses have you found helpful?

CHAPTER 7

Why Do I Find It Hard to Trust God?

Many people tend to have a wrong concept of what God is like. Wrong perceptions of God keep us from being comforted by the God of all comfort and hinder us from trusting Him who is worthy of our trust. As long as we have doubts about God's goodness, we can't find comfort in the truth that everything that comes our way comes from Him—that it is, in fact, Father-filtered.

So before we attempt to answer in some small measure the question "What is God like?", let us uncover some of our blind spots, some of our unconscious ideas about what God is like. What we actually think God is like and how we think He feels toward us is one of the biggest reasons we don't draw close to Him and find our security in Him. That's one of the reasons we struggle. We don't really know Him. And most of the time that's why we find it difficult to trust Him.

JUDGING GOD BECAUSE OF ONE EVENT

Often we single out an experience and say, "If God is really God, why doesn't He do something about all the pain and problems of the world?"

Whether consciously or unconsciously, we read into some single action of God toward us the motives and attitudes which are not His, but are our dreamed-up ideas. We can't base our understanding of God—or anyone—on one event. We can wonder why God allowed the event, but if we focus on that isolated situation, we forget all of His past goodness and His promise that His plans are "for good not for disaster, to give you a future and a hope" (Jer. 29:11).

Allowing God to be God is hard for us. We may have difficulty:

- letting Him call the shots.
- letting Him order our circumstances according to His timing.
- being satisfied with His choices.
- trusting Him in the midst of devastating events without fully understanding their purpose.

From our limited view, we can develop the perception that God is unkind, unwise, uncaring, or unable to do anything to change the situation.

We may compare God to imperfect humans and think that . . .

God is a busy, uninvolved parent: "He's too busy and doesn't have time for me. People don't have time for me, and God doesn't either. He has the whole universe to care for. I shouldn't bother Him with my petty concerns and needs."

He will fail as people do: "He will fail me just like everyone else. How could I possibly be important enough for Him to take an interest in? He is no different from the humans who have failed me."

He doesn't understand me: "I have unique problems that He does not understand. I'm the exception—my weaknesses, my temperament, my terrible background. I'm different. He doesn't understand me."

He is a partial parent: "He's good to others, but He isn't good to me. Good things always happen to others, but things like that don't happen to me."

He is an accusing parent: "He is a harsh judge and enjoys making me feel guilty and miserable when I do wrong. He just waits to punish me for messing up."

I should be strong enough on my own: "It's a weakness in me if I have to go to God with my needs. I should be strong and be able to handle life on my own."

God is a perfectionist parent: "I have to earn His favor. I feel I must earn His love by being good and by increasing my prayers and Bible study. I'm afraid that I am not quite good enough for Him to accept me."

People have disappointed us, betrayed us, used us, or abused us, and we may have learned we cannot trust them. We tend to make God out of the same mold and materials. Many times these impressions come from the way our parents have treated us or are implications drawn from our experiences with them or other authority figures. But God is vastly different because He is limitless in His compassionate love. He knows no bounds in His patience. He knows no growth, nor does He diminish in anything that He is because He is complete. We are the opposite. We are finite beings and can't possibly fully comprehend Him. As Isaiah 40:25 says, "'To whom will you compare me? Who is my equal?' asks the Holy One." We must resist comparing God and Jesus to human beings, because "the Son radiates God's own glory and expresses the very character of God" (Heb. 1:3). The only person who shows us what God is really like is Jesus Christ, who came to reveal the Father.

Hannah Whitall Smith, in *The God of All Comfort*, writes of God's nature:

Because we do not know Him, we naturally get all sorts of wrong ideas about Him. We think He is an angry Judge who is on the watch for our slightest faults, or a harsh Taskmaster determined to exact from us the uttermost service, or a self-absorbed Deity demanding His full measure of honor and glory, or a far-off Sovereign concerned only with His own affairs and indifferent to our welfare. Who can wonder that such a God can neither be loved nor trusted? [1]

We can readily see that these ideas are diametrically opposed to what Jesus Christ was like. Jesus came to reveal the Father. He was God "manifest in the flesh." We see in Jesus the "express image" of God, and anything that is contrary to the life, words, and ways of Jesus is not true of God the Father.

TAKING A STAND ON TRUTH ABOUT GOD

After becoming aware of the wrong ideas we have had about God, we need to consider what He is really like and deliberately choose to believe what God says about His person—what He tells us He is like.

One way to do this is to read through the Gospels, taking special notice of what Jesus is like—His manner and attitude toward people and how He treats the weak and the sinful. Make notes of what you find and review these periodically. If we are going to experience the comfort of God's loving control, we must learn what kind of Father He really is. We need to deliberately and consistently take a stand on the truth about Him and refuse to entertain any thoughts that are at variance with this truth.

To acknowledge and then appropriately deal with thoughts, questions, and doubts about the person of God can be a healthy exercise that leads to a more solid faith. To be tempted to question God's goodness is not wrong, and although it may simply be a part of the human condition, questioning God can also be from Satan. However, even when the temptation comes from Satan, the temptation itself is not sin, as Jesus was tempted by Satan and yet He did not sin. In fact, many well-known people in the Bible, including King David and John the Baptist, had questions, but they did the right thing with their questions—they brought them to God. It's what we do with our questions and doubts on a continuing basis that is important.

When our honest questions lead to charges against God, we will find it harder and harder to trust in God's loving control. It is possible to embrace the truth about the character of God and still have some feelings of wonder, frustration, confusion, and struggle. We shouldn't deny or suppress those feelings. However, to have feelings of resentment toward God for not changing things or for not answering our prayers in our way or our timing is a sinful reaction that keeps us from peace. These feelings then need to be dealt with.

As we replace our wrong thoughts with new, true thoughts about God, we will find that our minds and hearts have a different outlook on the circumstances around us. Romans 12:2 says, "Let God transform you into a new person by changing the way you think." This is an ongoing process and is not accomplished in a day!

WHAT DOES THE PROCESS LOOK LIKE?

The psalmist David is a good example of someone who practiced the process of standing on truth by talking to himself. In Psalm 103:1–2 he admonishes himself, "Let all that I am praise the Lord; with my whole heart, I will praise his holy name. Let all that I am praise the Lord; may I never forget the good things he does for me." David even puts into words what he knows God to be like:

O Lord, you are so good, so ready to forgive, so full of unfailing love for all who ask for your help. (Psa. 86:5)

O Lord God of Heaven's Armies! Where is there anyone as mighty as you, O Lord? You are entirely faithful. (Psa. 89:8)

This I declare about the Lord: He alone is my refuge, my place of safety; he is my God and I trust him. (Psa. 91:2)

Even though David trusted God, he also brought his honest doubts and questions before God. Psalm 22 continues for twenty-one verses with a complaining plea for the Lord to see David's dire situation. Then beginning in verse 22, David breaks out in praise that God has heard, the kingdom is His, and He is to be praised. When our questions lead us to biblical truths about God, these questions are good and provide a catalyst for growth.

We don't only need to know what is true about God, but we also need to know God personally.[2] We need to cultivate a deeper relationship with Him. This is the believer's lifelong pursuit. We turn now to a brief look at our loving, compassionate God, who is worthy of our trust.

MAKE IT PERSONAL

1. Review the wrong thoughts about God (listed above) that many people typically have, and ask God to make clear to you which of these ideas you have been unconsciously entertaining. If you don't identify with any of these, in a quiet time of thoughtful meditation and prayer, ask the Lord to reveal to you any misconceptions that you may have.

2. From the Word of God, what is our counterattack when we are tempted to think of God as:

    Unfair: Deuteronomy 32:3–4

    Unwise: Daniel 2:20

    Unloving: 1 John 4:9–10

    Unkind: Titus 3:4

    Inattentive: Psalm 55:16–17

    Uncaring: 1 Peter 5:7

    Unable: 2 Corinthians 9:8

3. Write out your own words and a specific Scripture verse that will refute the wrong thoughts you have about God. Do this for each one you have listed. For example, Psalm 145:9, "The Lord is good to everyone," helps refute the wrong thought, "God is like a partial parent."

CHAPTER 8

God Is Good and God Is Love

To live with peace and joy in this sometimes unpleasant and hurtful world, we need to know that God is trustworthy, and we should have a deepening understanding of His loving, compassionate nature. To do this, we must contemplate the various aspects of His character.

More than anything else, we need to discover the love God has for us. God's unfailing love exists whether we know it or not, but we do not experience the comfort that comes from it unless we discover it for ourselves. There is no reluctance on His part to reveal His love, and we can have the joy of the continual discovery of His love for us. In discovering God's love, we are developing the habit of meeting all our difficulties and anxieties, as well as all our fears and perplexities, with the solid, eternal truth of God's loving care. First John 4:16 illustrates this free, unprompted love: "We know how much God loves us, and we have put our trust in his love."

GOD'S LOVE IS FREE AND UNPROMPTED

As humans, we tend to love someone we consider of value. Something in the other person prompts us or draws us to love them. Too often we think of God's love as being similar to our love for one another, but His love is vastly different in origin. God's love originates in Himself and is a self-caused, free, unprompted love. Not a single one of us called or prompted God to exercise His love toward us, because

His love is simply an expression of His great heart. That God loves us is what gives us value. He says to His people, Israel: "The Lord did not set his heart on you and choose you because you were more numerous than other nations, for you were the smallest of all nations! Rather, it was simply that the Lord loves you" (Deut. 7:7–8). John also writes about God's love: "This is real love—not that we loved God, but that he loved us and sent his Son as a sacrifice to take away our sins" (1 John 4:10).

Furthermore, God's love is more than His heart-love for us. His love encompasses His entire being. The Scripture says, "God is love" (1 John 4:8), and since God is love, it's a part of His nature to spontaneously, freely love with a love that encompasses each one of us personally and individually, no matter how unlovely we are or feel ourselves to be.

God's love doesn't depend on whether we measure up to certain expectations or whether we have given a proper response to His love. God does not portion out His love according to our devotion to Him, to our successes and failures in living out godly lives, or even according to the hours we spend in prayer or reading the Word. This free, unearned, unprompted love of God is one of the most comforting and rest-producing truths in the Bible. If we know that nothing in us or in our behavior drew out His love for us, then our actions will never cause Him to love us any less or turn His love away from us, because His love is unconditional, measureless, and limitless.

Of course, there are some requirements, some conditions, that will determine whether we, as God's children, will sense His love for us and whether we are able to find comfort in His love. When we sin against Him—or disobey Him—we put up a blockade so that we can't sense His love. In these situations, we may not feel His love, but God has not changed. He still loves us, a fact that never changes, even if we never repent. Nothing we say or do—or don't do—can change His love toward us. When we do repent, however, and turn back to God, we are able to experience anew the comfort of His everlasting, undiminishing, and complete love.[1]

EVERLASTING, UNDIMINISHING, COMPLETE LOVE

God loves us with an everlasting love. Since He has loved us from eternity, before time began, His love would have to be self-generated. Love was in God's very nature from before people existed.[2] God loved us when we were loveless, before we had any love for Him, which couldn't possibly be influenced by our actions or who we are now. God's love has always been what it is, and since it is everlasting, His love will never be diminished by our behaviors, thoughts, or performances—or the lack of them. Likewise, God's love for us can't grow any greater because it is as great, vast, and deep as ever could be possible. We can go deeper into the comfort of His love for us, but His love itself will not change because His love is a perfect and complete love from the beginning.

Even in all of life's varying circumstances, we can rest on the solid fact that God loves us! We can be absolutely certain about His relentless love for us. We can be certain of this when we fail, when we feel weak, and when we're disappointed or even disgusted with ourselves. God will not turn away from us or condemn us; our position before Him is unchanging, and therefore His response to us is only good. The Bible likens God's love for us to a loving father who demonstrates love for his child through his compassion and his loving discipline.

GOD'S UNFAILING GOODNESS

Perhaps we don't think God is always good to us. A critical question to ask ourselves is, "Do we believe God is good?" No doubt most of us would quickly answer, "Yes, of course!" If we were to probe a bit deeper, we could also ask, "Do we believe that He is *always* good?" and we may stop and think before answering with hesitation, ". . . Yes."

But do you believe God is *always* good to *you*? If we are honest and ready to admit some of our gut feelings, we may feel He is not always good to us. It's only human to have such thoughts, especially in the face of the confusing realities of life. In the full light of the Holy Spirit, it's a good idea to drag out our secret thoughts, doubts, or questions about God's goodness and love. As we face our inner feelings and questions with straight-up honesty, the answers can help us move toward our goal of aligning our inaccurate thoughts about God with truth, allowing us to choose the faith way, believing against our contrary feelings. If left unchecked, our wrong thoughts tend to create a gap that grows too wide for us to see His true character.

Psalm 119:68 says, "You are good and do only good." God is never bad, nor does He do bad things. But we may wonder what "good" truly means. Certainly it is the opposite of bad. If God were unkind or indifferent to, or even neglectful of, my needs, He would not be good. On the positive side, to be good is to continually live up to the highest and best that we know. Since God is omniscient, He always knows what is best, and since He is good, without failure He lives up to the highest and best there is. The Word of God indisputably affirms that God is good: "O Lord, you are so good, so ready to forgive, so full of unfailing love for all who ask for your help" (Psa. 86:4–5), and "The Lord is good, a strong refuge when trouble comes. He is close to those who trust in him" (Nahum 1:7).

DO WE REALLY BELIEVE GOD IS GOOD?

There will be times in our lives when we may not really believe that God is good, even though we know He is good and works every situation for our good. Here are some questions we can ask ourselves to check how deeply we believe in God's goodness and lovingkindness for us. If I really believe God loves and cares for me:

- Why do I grumble or become discontent over the circumstances God allows to come to me?

- Why am I distrustful or anxious about the future?
- Why don't I thank Him more for the good things in my life?
- How quick am I to question God's goodness in the face of pain and misery?

Our understanding of God's goodness will be enhanced if we remember two aspects of His goodness. The first is the revealed goodness of God where it is declared in His Word. He has given us a multitude of examples of the outworking of His goodness in the lives of biblical characters, allowing us to see His goodness in our own life experiences.

The second is the mysterious goodness of God when we can't see His face or understand what He is doing. The promise of Romans 8:28 does not mean we will be able to trace His hand in these experiences, but we can trust Him as we wait for His explanations and reflect on who He is, praising Him for His character and His name. This is where we have to walk by faith, believing the Word of God is true when it says that God is good and does good and is all powerful, even though our finite minds have such limited understanding.

MAKE IT PERSONAL

1. Take the comfort of God's love for yourself by receiving the truths in these verses. To do this, first describe His love, then write a sentence expressing your faith in His love for you. See Romans 5:8, Romans 8:31–39, and Ephesians 2:4–7.

2. Think of a time when you were depressed, discouraged, or anxious. Can you relate that to questioning and doubting God's goodness at that time?

3. What are some things loving parents do for their child to show love when the child is feeling disappointed, rejected, confused, doesn't understand, or has even failed? The Bible says we can compare God's love for His children to a loving parent's love, except God's love is much more (Matt. 5:7–11.)

CHAPTER 9

Unoffended by the Unexplained

One of the most fundamental questions we wrestle with is why a good God allows suffering in this world. How many times has the question been asked, "If God is indeed good and is in control, why does He allow bad things to happen to good people?" As we try to reconcile this question in our minds, it seems that either He doesn't have the power to change things or He doesn't care, and therefore, He is not good. Human reasoning says God cannot both be good and also allow suffering. Then we get offended by the pain in this life when we misunderstand what God has promised, that He is both loving and in control.

To better understand God's loving control, we must remind ourselves of some of the things already covered in this book. First, when something bad happens, it does not mean that God caused it to happen. This would give us free rein to blame God for all the tragedies and problems in our own lives and in the world, including rapes, incest, muggings, fatal accidents, divorce, and family violence, which would mean that God is *not* a good God. Second, God doesn't cause a tragic circumstance so that He can then bring good out of it. This is not God's way. To say that God can bring good things out of bad situations is quite different from saying that God causes tragic things to happen *because* of the good that can come out of them.

If we know that God is sovereign, we also know that God, in His sovereignty, has placed us in a world of sin and suffering from which we have no immunity. The fact that millions of Africans are starving is not good, a crippling or terminal disease is not pleasant, nor is a broken marriage a desirable thing. As mentioned earlier, these things enter my life, even though I am a committed Christian. I must therefore acknowledge that God is in control and that He will give me grace and strength to endure whatever pain I am going through.

Just because we are Christians experiencing God's loving control doesn't mean He allows only good things to happen to us, His people. Christians obviously share in the pain and sorrow and death that is part of our world system. Christians suffer from accidents, from disease, from rejection, and from painful relationships. In fact, Jesus told us to expect difficult lives. John 16:33 declares, "Here on earth you will have many trials and sorrows. But take heart, because I have overcome the world." As Christians we are not exempt, but we have a greater support in Jesus, a God who has experienced the sufferings of this world and understands our pain, and we have His Spirit, who gives us power to cope and a purpose to believe in (see Heb. 4:15.)

We can experience the comfort in knowing that God loves us with an everlasting love, He counts the very hairs on our heads, and He is moving toward the fulfillment of His marvelous plan for our lives. He is the God whose own Son hung and died on a cross. He is not a God far off, but rather is near and deeply involved in the big and little events of our lives.

TRUSTING HIM IN THE UNEXPLAINED

Sometimes we face circumstances for which God never provides an explanation. The Bible tells us about John the Baptist, who reached out to Jesus from prison. Undoubtedly anticipating his fate, a likely execution, John sent his disciples to Jesus to ask if He really was the Messiah.

Maybe underlying John's question were his real questions: If You really are the Messiah, why have You left me here in this dark, damp cell? Why haven't You made every effort to free me? Why have You not sent me any words of comfort? Do You not care about me?

Instead of directly answering John's question, Jesus responded, "This, John, is what's happening. The blind see and the lame walk; the lepers are cleansed and the deaf hear; the dead are raised up and the poor have the gospel preached to them." In effect, He was telling John's messengers, "Tell John what I am doing. He's right. I do have all power. I may not be delivering him in the way he expected, but tell him to trust Me now with the unexplained."

Like John, we will never fully understand God's ways or be able to give precise reasons for all His acts, because God's "thoughts are nothing like your thoughts,' says the Lord. 'And my ways are far beyond anything you could imagine" (Isa. 55:8–9). We can make a choice, by faith, to trust in His loving control and in His goodness, because His ways and thoughts are perfect no matter how many times we wrestle with the unexplained in our situations.

WRESTLING WITH THE UNEXPLAINED

Often when we are deeply shaken, a flood of questions confronts us. "Why did God let this . . .? Why didn't He change . . .? Why do I have to go through . . .? " These are sometimes hard, unanswerable questions. Elisabeth Elliot writes:

There would be no sense in asking "why?" if one did not believe in anything. The word itself presupposes purpose. Purpose presupposes a purposeful intelligence. Somebody has to have been responsible. It is because we believe in God that we address questions to Him. We believe that He is just and that He is love, but that belief is put to severe strain as we wrestle with our pains and perplexities, with our very position in His ordered universe.[1]

We have heard the argument that it is a bad thing to ask God why or question what He is doing. Actually, the question can be either good or bad. As mentioned earlier, if we ask with a closed fist held up toward God in a spirit of rebellion, resistance, accusation, or unbelief, then the question is a destructive thing. But if we ask with an open hand, in sincere faith, with an honest desire of cooperating with God as He accomplishes His good purposes in our lives, to learn all that we can from the situation and to grow in grace through it, then it is a valuable and helpful question.

God is delighted when His children ask Him their honest questions—even those who, in the midst of pain, ask in a spirit of doubt. He will not deal with these questions impatiently or harshly; instead, he lovingly longs for his children to come again to the place of trusting.

He knows our frame and remembers we are dust.[2]

In his book *Where Is God When it Hurts?*, Philip Yancey writes:

I have been with sick Christian people who torment themselves with the question, "What is God trying to teach me?" Maybe they have it all wrong. Maybe God isn't trying to tell us anything specific each time we hurt. Pain and suffering are part and parcel of our planet, and Christians are not exempt. . . . As I look at the Bible, the evidence seems inconclusive. Sometimes God caused suffering for a specific reason— usually a warning. Sometimes Satan caused it. In other cases . . . God wasn't intending any specific message.[3]

In trying to rationalize what God is teaching us through our everyday circumstances, and even in the ones that shake us, we often cannot process what is happening to us. Such an event happened in Keisha's life.

Keisha's Story: *I always wanted to be a mother. At a young age, I had made the choice to follow Christ. I always knew that God had a plan for my life, and I wanted to follow it. I had already experienced some difficult situations in life, and also times where I had hard choices to make. God definitely used those times to bring me closer to Him, to depend on Him, to trust in Him, and ultimately to know Him more. My love for Him and faith in Him grew as a result. In my mind, I had always wondered if God's plan included me having children. I hoped more than anything that it would!*

My husband and I had been married four years when we started to try for our first baby. We were ecstatic when I quickly became pregnant, and we welcomed our son into the world. Every expectation I had had of motherhood was more than exceeded.

Shortly after our son turned one, we decided to try for another baby, and sure enough, I fell pregnant very quickly for the second time. We were again so thankful and excited about the direction our lives seemed to be taking.

However, a few weeks into this pregnancy, I experienced my first miscarriage. I was completely shocked and devastated. What was happening? I knew of others who had experienced this, but I was really taken by surprise. I remember thinking that this should not have been part of the plan for my life. I wanted answers to my pain. How could I try to stop the hurt and pain I was feeling? God knew this was my biggest desire! Why did this have to happen?

Looking back, I realize I had a big misunderstanding of suffering and God's part in it all. I avoided trusting this area of my life to God and tried to deal with my pain myself. Soon after the miscarriage, I became pregnant again. This time I was very fearful. I tried to predict what was going to happen, feared the worst, and wanted to control the situation myself. I was still very hurt and scared after the last time, and I didn't know how to trust God with this pregnancy. I was so overcome by my fears that there was no room in my heart for letting anyone else in. If I'm honest with myself, I thought if God really loved me, surely He would know I needed this baby to be okay.

A couple of weeks into the pregnancy, we were pretty sure things were not progressing well. We had been told that the baby wasn't growing as it should be, but we'd have to wait and see how things went. It was a matter of waiting. That was the longest six weeks of my life. Day after day I pleaded with God to change the situation and for things to be okay. As we went for each scan, I hoped for a miracle, for things to be exactly as they should. I knew how powerful God was—I had experienced Him at work in my life in many ways. This was one small thing He could take care of for me.

I couldn't understand what was going on. I remember thinking, What is God trying to teach me here? If there was something I needed to learn, I needed to do it quickly so that my life could change for the better.

Is God trying to tell us something? It may be dangerous, and perhaps even unscriptural, to torture ourselves by looking for His message. The message may simply be that, like everyone else, we live in a world with fixed laws. But from the larger view, from the view of all history, yes, God is speaking to us through pain—or perhaps in spite of pain. He can use it to make us aware of Him. Keisha's story continues:

At the end of my first trimester, I miscarried for the second time. I was done. I was exhausted and weary in every way. I had fought with God, ignored Him, and remained angry in my pain and hurt. And it was here that I came to God in my despair. I vividly remember crying out to Him.

I expressed my need for Him. I knew He was real and I knew that He loved me, but I felt so far away from Him at that point in time. I cried out to Him to come and help me because I knew there was nothing else that was going to get me through this. I didn't know how things were going to change. I was so lost. All I could do was turn to Ruth chapter 2, where it talks about taking refuge under the wings of the Lord. This very idea just brought me to my knees, and I cried and cried to God. I was giving Him my pain. For the first time in this whole time I was really letting Him in. I didn't know how it was all going to end up, but for now I was giving my pain to Him. God gave me such comfort in this idea of taking refuge in Him. He was my Father and I needed to trust in His loving care, and all I could do at that point was take refuge. My pain wasn't going away anytime soon, but He was the God in whom I could take refuge.[4]

DID GOD OWE JOB AN EXPLANATION?

Job met the onset of his troubles with a strong faith response: "The Lord gave me what I had, and the Lord has taken it away. Praise the name of the Lord!" (Job 1:21). But as time went on and his "friends" taunted, questioned, and accused him, confusion came creeping in: "My complaint today is still a bitter one, and I try hard not to groan aloud. If only I knew where to find God. . . . I go east, but he is not there. I go west, but I cannot find him" (Job 23:2–3, 8).

Didn't God owe Job an explanation as to why life had been so unfair? Instead of answering Job's specific questions, out of the whirlwind God poured out a flood of questions for Job to consider.

Where were you when I laid the foundations of the earth? Tell me, if you know so much. (Job 38:4)

Who kept the sea inside its boundaries as it burst from the womb? . . . I said, "This far and no farther will you come. Here your proud waves stop!" (Job 38:8, 11)

Can you direct the constellations through the seasons, or . . . make lightning appear and cause it to strike as you direct? (Job 38:32, 35)

God was essentially saying to Job, "Can you do any of this? I am the God who can do all of this. It's not so much answers to your questions that you need, but a fresh look at what I am like."

Job made a new response of faith. He chose to let God be God as he confessed:

I know that you can do anything, and no one can stop you. You asked "Who is this that questions my wisdom with such ignorance?" It is I—and I was talking about things I knew nothing about, things far too wonderful for me. . . . I had only heard about you before, but now I have seen you with my own eyes. I take back everything I said, and I sit in dust and ashes to show my repentance. (Job 42:2–3, 5–6)

God caused Job to realize something of His incomparable greatness in creation, and Job admitted there were things he would never understand. God didn't answer Job's questions; He revealed more of Himself.

JESUS DIDN'T ALWAYS ANSWER THE WHYS

There were times when Jesus explained mysteries and answered questions for the disciples, but there were other times when He gave no explanation. When Peter questioned Jesus washing his feet, Jesus's answer was, "What I am doing you do not understand now, but you will know after this." And when Peter wanted to know what was going to happen to John, Jesus did not explain, but rather reminded Peter that his responsibility was simply to follow Him.[5]

We could cite question after question that comes into our minds. Why did a young man in the prime of his life, with a young family and a vital ministry depending on him, suddenly collapse with a heart attack, while an elderly woman lies day after day needing continual nursing care, not able to communicate with loved ones, no longer a companion to her husband?

We all have times when we are overwhelmed with what seems to us to be an unexplained situation. You may never know why your child was born with physical and mental problems, or why your wife or husband died when your children were still toddlers, or why you remain single so long when you've prayed so faithfully for a partner, or why God didn't answer your prayer and keep the divorce from happening. God may be trusting you with the unexplained. The important thing is to receive the person or circumstance with that heart response of "Yes, Lord, You are in loving control of my life. I may not be able to understand why this has happened, but I can trust Your heart of love." No, God didn't promise an explanation for every trial, but He promises that:

When you go through deep waters, I will be with you. When you go through rivers of difficulty, you will not drown. When you walk through the fire of oppression, you will not be burned up; the flames will not consume you. For I am the Lord, your God, the Holy One of Israel, your Savior. . . . Do not be afraid, for I am with you . (Isa. 43:2–3, 5)

He gives us something better—the assurance that He will be with us and bring us through the difficulties as we trust Him and commit ourselves to Him.

TRUSTING GOD IN THE DARK

Many of us may live our whole lives on this earth and never receive an explanation as to why we experienced such difficulties. Jesus says there are times when God will not lift the darkness from you, but trust Him. God will appear like an unkind friend, but He is not. He will appear like an unnatural father, but He is not. He will appear like an unjust judge, but He is not. Keep growing in your understanding of God's character and His will. Nothing happens outside of God's loving control. Therefore, you can rest and have perfect confidence in Him.

If we choose to believe that God is good, then all that He does must be good, no matter how it looks. I can wait for His explanations. God promises us great reward in this life and the next (see Heb. 10:35–36). He understands our questions. It isn't that we won't have more questions, but if our questions keep us from trusting His goodness and wisdom, then we will end up forfeiting His peace. It is such a relief and a rest to know we can trust Him in the dark, unoffended by the unexplained, allowing us to say, "I may not understand, but I can trust."

MAKE IT PERSONAL

1. Make a concise list of some of the misunderstandings you may have about God's control. Does this help you better understand the pain and suffering in the world and in your world?

2. Is there something in your life now that appears to have no meaning and no purpose and seems to be a mystery of God's providence or mysterious ways? Do you have some confused or negative thoughts about God? Based on Psalm 62:8: "Pour out your heart to him," write out your feelings and thoughts to God. Express yourself freely. You won't offend Him.

3. Read Isaiah 43:2–5, Isaiah 50:10, and Isaiah 55:8–9. You may find it useful to write these verses out. After you have done so, write some expressions of faith to God. In your current circumstances, how will you choose to be unoffended by the unexplained?

CHAPTER 10

What Part Do I Play? Am I Just a Passive Puppet?

God's loving control doesn't remove our responsibility to take action. It doesn't mean it's okay to say, "God is in control, so there's nothing I can do." Many times there is something we can do. If I am struggling in my marriage, there are ways I can work through the struggle. If I've had a misunderstanding or disagreement with someone, there are steps I can take to resolve the problem. When we see suffering and injustice in the world, we can speak out or act.

In none of these cases do we sit back and passively assert, "Oh, God is in control. There's nothing I can do or need to do." Each day, we encounter circumstances that give us an opportunity to do something positive. As such, we continue to grow in our understanding of God's will by taking appropriate action and trusting that God is working in this and He will do what is best. However, we should not use this truth as a crutch for our laziness, lack of involvement, or lack of concern in a situation where we can accept responsibility and act, even if it may involve a little risk.

ACCEPTING RESPONSIBILITY AND TAKING RISKS

Adam and Julie had entered a downward spiral of conflict in their marriage. They seemed to be fighting about everything, and they both felt hopeless and were convinced it was the other person who had to change. Eventually they realized they needed the input and advice from others. With help, they accepted that they each had to take responsibility for their own attitudes and actions. As they asked God to reveal their own weaknesses and destructive behaviors and sought accountability from others, they saw the dynamics in their marriage improve.

As well as taking responsibility for the part we play in the difficulties we face and in overcoming them, we also need to determine whether we have a responsibility to act in order to help someone else. One of the ways we can do this is by speaking the truth in love, as Jenny has done.

Jenny's Story: *Jenny watched her friend—who for the majority of her life had denied the impact of her painful past—now start down the path of an eating disorder. Jenny could see how this disorder gave her friend a sense of control and distraction as she struggled to come to terms with her abuse and how God could have let it happen. Could Jenny passively watch her friend destroy her life and her body this way? Jenny had to decide if she should lovingly confront her friend, risking that her friend would reject her counsel, halt the progress she was making, and run away from those who could help her. Jenny made the choice to confront her friend. It was risky, and it was painful. Her friend responded well, and although there is still a long way to go, she is continuing to make progress to overcome her past.*

To take responsibility for the part we need to play in our own or others' struggles requires taking a risk. The end result may not be as positive as the illustration here because there is no guarantee things will work out as we would hope, but we play our part by trusting that God will do what is best in our situation.

I'M RESPONSIBLE FOR MY MIND

As we are trusting God to do what is best in our situations, it's our responsibility to fill our minds and hearts with God's Word, especially about His character, as mentioned in chapters 7 and 8. When you became a Christian, God did not remove the old pattern of wrong thinking and replace it with a new one that never requires any effort of change on our part. Romans 12:2 NIV says we should no longer be conformed to the pattern of this world, but instead should be transformed by the renewing of our minds, and through that transformation we will know what the will of God is. If we are going to be comforted by our loving God, we have to discard our old wrong thoughts about Him and fill our minds with biblical truth as to what He is really like. This is not a quick, overnight exchange, but is a lifelong discipline, a constant process, and a daily responsibility.

I'M RESPONSIBLE FOR MY PRAYERS

Just as we are responsible for our own thoughts, we are also responsible for the part we play and how we respond to God working in our lives. A common question when things are not going the way we planned is, "If God is allowing this to happen, why do I need to pray, asking Him to change a person or a circumstance?" How can we reconcile these two seemingly opposing concepts? God is sovereign, yet He has chosen to include us in His plan to reach the world.

One way we play our part is through prayer. James understood God's desire for His children to ask, when he wrote to the scattered Jewish Christians, "You do not have because you do not ask" (James 4:2 NIV). If God did not want us to ask, why would He make such promises as, "You can ask for anything in my name, and I will do it, so that the Son can bring glory to the Father. Yes, ask me for anything in my name, and I will do it!" (John 14:13–14)?

Jesus taught His disciples the need to pray, "Your will be done on earth as it is in heaven." This means that God has chosen to limit some of His activities in response to the prayers of His people. Unless they pray, He will not act. Heaven may will something to happen, but heaven waits and encourages earth's initiative to desire that will, and then to will and pray that it happens. The will of God is not done on earth by an all-powerful force overriding or ignoring the will of man on earth. On the contrary, God has willed that His hand be held back while He waits for you, the intercessor, to pray, "Your will be done on earth (in this or that specific situation)."[1]

PRAYER COUPLED WITH ACCEPTANCE

Prayer coupled with acceptance is essential in spiritual warfare. There is a battle raging in the heavenly realms. Ephesians 6 charges us to put on the armor and pray! God is the One who tears down Satan's strongholds and defeats the enemy, and prayer is a vital part of those victories won. In 2 Corinthians 12:7–10 we see the apostle Paul praying for God to deliver him from a particular struggle he was facing. Paul calls it his "thorn in the flesh." God's answer was to give Paul grace for his weakness, and Paul was to be content with God's will.

On the night before His death, Jesus prayed in earnest that the cup of His suffering might be taken away, but despite His anguish, He was able to say, "Not my will, but yours be done." He was willing to accept what God was allowing, but that did not keep Him from praying for deliverance. With both Jesus and Paul, it seems there was a point in which they stopped praying for relief and simply rested in the will of God.

There are certainly references in the Bible that speak of praying for restored health and relief from trials. The prayers Paul wrote to the various churches concentrated on God developing their character rather than providing relief from undesirable circumstances or people. To the church at Philippi, Paul wrote:

Not that I was ever in need, for I have learned how to be content with whatever I have. I know how to live on almost nothing or with every-

thing. I have learned the secret of living in every situation, whether it is with a full stomach or empty, with plenty or little. For I can do everything through Christ, who gives me strength. (Phil. 4:11–13)

Yet this prayer also applies to us in our situations. Paul's emphasis seems to be about asking for and receiving God's marvelous grace and strength to endure, persevere, and glorify Him in the midst of our difficulties and troubles.

WE CAN'T MAKE IT ALONE

It is important to realize we cannot maintain the right balance between playing our part through prayer, action, and trusting in God, and also trusting in our own strength. We need the Holy Spirit's help. In Jesus's last conversation with His disciples, He tells them it is better that He leaves them because the Holy Spirit will come. In John 14 and 15 Jesus explains the role the Holy Spirit will have in our lives as our advocate, our helper, and our comforter. The Holy Spirit assures us personally of the Father's love and reminds us of what we have learned, and He shows us how to apply it to our lives and circumstances. Jesus says the disciples should not let their hearts be troubled. The disciples were not alone, and neither are we if we have accepted Christ and have His Spirit within us.

Later on in the New Testament, Paul explains the fruit that comes from the Spirit's work in our lives. Galatians 5:22–23 says the fruit of the Spirit is love, joy, peace, patience, kindness, goodness, faithfulness, gentleness, and self-control. The Spirit will cultivate these things in our lives as we cooperate with Him.

God is bigger than any person or circumstance that impacts our lives. When we acknowledge His control, we are not saying that we then sit back and do nothing. God has given us free will, which is the actual freedom to choose, and He has provided the indwelling Holy

Spirit who, as we cooperate with Him and draw upon His strength, enables us to take responsible steps of action and respond with gratitude.

MAKE IT PERSONAL

1. The Christian life is a life of faith. We are constantly told to believe, rest, and trust. Our new life springs from God, not from anything in us (2 Corinthians 5:17). Fill in the blanks with the words that describe what God does for us, as found in the verses provided.

    It is God who_____. Philippians 2:13

    It is God who_____. Philippians 4:7

    It is God who_____. Philippians 4:13

    It is God who_____. Philippians 4:19

2. We are also given some clear directives as to things we are to do. Describe those you find in Colossians 3:1–17.

3. Describe a current problem for which you need wisdom and direction. What part of it is totally out of your control? Is there anything about it you can change? (Sometimes the only action we can take is to pray and choose a new response of commitment and trust.)

CHAPTER 11

Attitude, Gratitude

An attitude of gratitude is a major ingredient in letting the truth of God's loving control work in our lives. The clear and challenging command from 1 Thessalonians 5:18 is, "Be thankful in all circumstances, for this is God's will for you who belong to Christ Jesus." There are very few times in the Bible when God spells out His will so specifically. Perhaps He knew this would be a hard one for us.

BEING THANKFUL IN EVERYTHING

There is one big question that arises out of Ephesians 5:20 about giving "thanks always and for everything to God the Father in the name of our Lord Jesus Christ" (ESV). Some people maintain that this teaches we must give thanks for all things that come into our lives, whatever their origin. Does God actually want me to thank Him for my friend being killed in a car accident, a child getting cancer, or a wife cheating on her husband? If so, I am being asked to give thanks for evil.

Actually, the very opposite is true. Because of the evil in the world and in ourselves, Jesus had to come and die a terrible death in order that we could be forgiven and restored to a right relationship with God. How could we be asked to give thanks for something that cost Jesus His life? For example, Romans 8:19–24 tells us that all creation looks forward to the day that it will be free from the effects of sin, death, and decay in this world. Rather than being thankful for sin and suffering, it's as if we are experiencing labor pains, waiting to be delivered from these terrible things.

Commentators point out that these verses teach us we are to be thankful *in* all circumstances, not *for* all circumstances. God does not ask us to give thanks for anything related to the sin and evil of this world, but He tells us to give thanks *in* all of our circumstances. What does this actually mean?

Even when the situation is bad or seemingly hopeless, we can always thank God for His love, His wisdom, and His care for us in all things. In this case, "thank you" becomes an expression of faith. As previously discussed, although God may not have ordered the event in our lives, we can thank Him that even this was filtered through His love and grace. Although the circumstance itself may not be the will of God, by the time it comes to me it has become the permissive will of God, and at that point I must accept that it came from Him and not from a secondary cause. God is there to compel this event or these people in my life to work together for my good. We do not thank God for the suffering, but we give thanks to the Lord in the midst of the suffering.

Giving thanks is the expression of my confident trust that God is too wise to make any mistakes and too loving to be unkind in His dealings with me, so that:

when you have three boys and you want a girl so badly . . .

when you are unable to have children . . .

when you've had enough of the loneliness of being single . . .

when you are in the middle of a messy divorce . . .

when you discover your young teenager is using drugs . . .

when the boss expects more overtime and you're already stressed out . . .

when health issues mean you can't do all the things you want to . . .

there is a proper spirit of gratitude for times like these. It is based on the character of God and springs from the assurance that God is who He claims to be, and that "the Lord will withhold no good thing from those who do what is right" (Psa. 84:11). It is a confidence that He loves us and is making no mistakes. That is real faith!

HOW DISCONTENT IS EXPRESSED

Having real faith involves learning to habitually walk in this attitude of gratitude that is independent of circumstances and people. Some of us may have more to unlearn than others in this regard. Many people are temperamentally inclined to see the glass as always half empty. They can easily see what will go wrong or the flaw in the plan, and they will be the first to complain.

The opposite of a spirit of gratitude is a spirit of complaint. Mixed with that is deep discontentment, which is expressed in finding fault—with our circumstances, with God, with the people in our world. Sometimes we discreetly label this "discernment," when actually we are rehearsing the shortcomings of people and censuring God's ways. It's hard to call it what it really is—a discontentment with God's ways.

We find this discontentment in the Bible. Even though God delivered the Israelites from slavery in Egypt, time and time again they grumbled about what God had provided for them or what He didn't provide. They grumbled about their water. They grumbled about their food. They grumbled against Moses and Aaron, their leaders. Moses called it by its real name when he said, "Your complaints are against the Lord, not against us" (Ex. 16:8).

The Psalmist tells us that when the Lord heard the complaining of His people, His anger came up against them "for they did not believe God or trust him to care for them" (Psa. 78:22). The bottom line is that all complaining means that we are not trusting God.

In contrast, an attitude of gratitude is evidence that we are living by faith and trusting in the goodness of the Lord. Tracing God's steps in our lives gives us cause for praise and thanksgiving. He is Lord! He is not only Lord of my adversity, but He is Lord of my prosperity. We need to recognize that whatever is good and perfect is a gift coming down to us from God our Father (James 1:17).

Thanking God in advance for His promised grace to help in time of need is faith, and faith in God is built on God's faithfulness in the past through the sureness of His Word, the solidness of His character, the perfect fulfillment of His promises, and His unending provision for our needs. By remembering God's faithfulness in the past, we enlarge our faith for present needs, prepare for the uncertainties of the future, and build good habits in the good times so we are better able to give thanks when trials do come.

The Bible is full of descriptions of people who were reminded of God's past faithfulness and goodness toward them as they faced uncertain futures. In God's dealings with Israel, after any major triumph or event, He told them to build a stone memorial. For example, after crossing the Jordan River, they built a twelve-stone memorial that was to serve as a reminder of what God had done. If He was able to work mightily in their lives through the big things, then they could trust Him for tomorrow too (Josh. 4:20–24). People from Moses to David to Mary to Paul all understood the importance of facing difficult circumstances or suffering from a position of thankfulness to God for His faithfulness to them in the past. Through those experiences, they were assured that God would be faithful to them in the future.

MAKE IT PERSONAL

1. What attitude is the opposite of gratitude?
2. Can you think of a recent situation in which you found it difficult to obey the command "in everything give thanks"? Describe your experience. What did you choose to do?
3. What is the difference between "in everything give thanks" and giving thanks "for everything"?

4. No matter our circumstances, we can still give thanks to God. What do these verses teach us to give thanks for? Write down your answers.

> Romans 6:17–18
>
> 2 Thessalonians 1:3
>
> 1 Timothy 1:12
>
> Psalm 107:1–2
>
> John 6:11

CHAPTER 12

The Bottom Line

The purpose of this book has been to answer the question, Can we trust God? We have seen that God is in fact good, and His goodness to us is constant and unending, even when difficult circumstances enter our lives. God is faithful and keeps His promises. His promise to us is that He will work everything together for our good as we continue to trust in His will for our lives.

But we don't decide to trust God only when difficulties come our way. In order to be able to trust in Him during difficult times, we must learn to trust Him every day of our lives. This means trusting God to meet our fundamental needs.

WHAT ARE OUR BASIC NEEDS?

All human beings, of course, have practical needs that must be met. Food and shelter are examples of these. But as creatures made in the image of God, we have fundamental needs that go beyond the physical. A variety of words have been used, but a simple, comprehensive description is acceptance, security, and significance. All I really need in life for satisfaction and fulfillment is acceptance, security, and significance. It sounds so simple, yet it becomes so complex.

To be accepted means to be loved and approved for who I really am without fear of rejection. As human beings, we yearn for acceptance and fear being rejected. Most of us look for acceptance from other people. This may lead to hiding who we really are or trying to become someone we think others will accept.

We have been programmed to believe that security is owning our own home, having a permanent job, and having enough savings in the bank. Our security also includes a loving family and friends. The problem is that we can never have enough money in the bank to feel secure, and we try to control every aspect of our lives, including our relationships.

Significance is more personalized, and therefore more elusive. Depending on our backgrounds or personalities, we look for significance and respect in different ways. Usually it boils down to the feelings of self-worth around the contributions we are making and how others view our contributions.

So if these are God-given needs, how does God plan for these needs to be met? From whom or what do we derive our ultimate satisfaction? We may be quick to respond that Jesus is all we need, and "this same God who takes care of me will supply all your needs from his glorious riches, which have been given to us in Christ Jesus" (Phil. 4:19). We have no trouble declaring the sufficiency of Christ, but is that where we are actually looking to have our needs met?

Most of us behave as if people, events, and circumstances are the things that will bring us fulfillment. When events and circumstances are good and going my way, or when people are responding to me with love and appreciation, I feel accepted, secure, and significant. But what happens when people reject me, fail me, or ignore me? Where do I turn when my circumstances are out of my control and life seems to be falling apart? It is usually not until we have exhausted all other sources that we are forced to find how adequate God Himself is to meet our needs.

WHAT PART DO PEOPLE PLAY?

If the truth is that I need nothing but God and what He chooses to provide for my everyday needs, where do people fit into my life? Are we not to love, encourage, and care for one another? Larry Crabb, author of *Basic Principles of Biblical Counseling*, says:

Restricting dependency to God does not, however, minimize the importance and desirability of human relationships. It is right and normal to derive a wonderful sense of security from the love and fellowship of a spouse, friends, of brothers and sisters in Christ. When God blesses me with the love of other people, I am to respond gratefully by enjoying their love and basking in the security it brings. But I am to recognize that my deepest need for security is now being met and always will be met by an eternal, unchanging God of love. If loved ones turn on me, if I am placed in a situation where warm fellowship is unavailable, I am to aggressively believe that the biblical route to meeting my security needs is to recognize that the sovereign God of the universe loves me. He is all that I need because He will arrange my world down to every minute detail (to believe that requires belief in a big God) in such a way that all my most basic needs will be met if I trust Him. Therefore, whatever happens to me, whether insults, loss of love, rejection, snubbing, or not being invited to a certain social gathering, I am to respond with the rational, trusting response of thanksgiving.

Therefore, it is in and through God Himself we can find our ultimate satisfaction to meet our needs, whatever they may be.[1]

If God is all we need, then we can simply trust Him, because He is our abundant need and ultimate satisfaction.

FINDING ULTIMATE SATISFACTION

We consistently slip into the habit of looking for these needs to be met in all the wrong places. Instead, God wants us to turn to Him. He will accomplish this by shaking our self-sufficiency, our independence, and our reliance on possessions, health, children, or ministries. His shaking of our circumstances is always out of love, that we might be moved to find our needs all the more abundantly met in Him.

In fact, there are only two unshakable things: God and His Word. The list of the shakable is more complex. Even the mere admission that these things are temporary and fleeting brings a wave of uncertainty like a dark cloud over our souls. What if every shakable thing were taken away today—possessions, comforts, conveniences, meaningful work, social position, financial security, or even our family and friends? We would be reduced to the bottom line that our ultimate satisfaction is in God. We must each come to the place David did when he wrote, "I wait quietly before God, for my victory comes from him. He alone is my rock and my salvation, my fortress where I will never be shaken" (Psa. 62:1–2).

The basis for peace at the bottom line is absolute confidence in and loyalty to our Lord and full commitment to His will. If my purpose and my goals in life don't line up with this, but rather are to fulfill selfish ends that never satisfy, then I will tend to question the events of my life instead of seeing them as under God's control. Life will be centered around complaint instead of contentment.

The apostle Paul had a different attitude when facing distressing circumstances. He wrote, "But my life is worth nothing to me unless I use it for finishing the work assigned me by the Lord Jesus—the work of telling others the Good News about the wonderful grace of God" (Acts 20:24). Paul's purpose aligned with God's purpose—to finish his ministry of faithfully giving out the good news of the gospel. Because his will was one with the will of God, Paul could say, "None of my circumstances are shaking me." He was resting in the unshakable One.

Jesus is the ultimate example of surrendering our wills to God in that He has "come down from heaven to do the will of God who sent me, not to do my own will" (John 6:38). He never faltered in His faith in God's loving control, and even when facing the crucifixion, Jesus said, "My Father! If it is possible, let this cup of suffering be taken away from me. Yet I want your will to be done, not mine" (Matt. 26:39).

The aim of this book has been to show that our God is a good God and that He is in loving control of everything. Hopefully, as you have read along, you have taken some steps to a new life of peace and greater usefulness in the purposes of God as you live in this shaken world. We hope you have begun to practice drawing closer to Him by making Him your first reference in every situation, seeing Him in everything, acknowledging His loving control, believing that the events of your life are all Father-filtered, and trusting Him with the unexplained.

Our core verse for this book has been Romans 8:28: "And we know that God causes everything to work together for the good of those who love God and are called according to his purpose." We pray that you come to fully trust in this amazing promise so you may experience the peace and joy God has for you in each and every circumstance of your life.

MAKE IT PERSONAL

1. List some of the places from where you tend to draw your fulfillment and satisfaction. Beside that list, make a list of things that are shakable and temporary. How do the lists compare?

2. What does "God's loving control" mean to you now? How has this truth made a difference in your response to events and people in your day-to-day life?

3. What concepts have been most helpful as you have read and studied through this book? How is your attitude changing in response to:

    Knowing that God is the loving controller of all things?

    Seeing God in everything?

    Making God your first reference?

    Trusting Him with the unexplained?

    Seeing events as Father-filtered?

FURTHER STUDY SECTION:

Going Deeper

CHAPTER 1: GOD KNOWS BEST

1. How did each of the following people express his or her commitment to God's will, and in what ways?

Noah: Genesis 6:9–22; Hebrews 11:7

Abraham: Genesis 12:1, 4; 22:1–19; Hebrews 11:8, 17–19

Moses: Hebrews 11:24–26

Eli: 1 Samuel 3:10–18

David: Psalm 25:4–5; 40:8; 119:14–16; 143:8–10

Solomon: Psalm 72:18–19; Proverbs 3:5–6

Mary: Luke 1:38

Jesus: Matthew 26:39; John 4:34; 5:30

Paul: Acts 20:24; 21:13–14; 2 Corinthians 12:7–10; Philippians 3:7–14

2. In these verses, what are some other clear areas of God's will for His children?

Galatians 5:13–14

Ephesians 5:17–22, 25, 33; 6:1–9

Colossians 1:9–12

1 Thessalonians 4:3–7; 5:18

1 Timothy 2:1–2

1 Peter 2:13–17

3. What are some of the benefits that are ours when we line up our will with God's will?

Exodus 14:14

Psalm 1:3

Psalm 119:1–2

John 7:17; 13:17; 15:10

Ephesians 6:2–3

1 John 3:22

CHAPTER 2: GOD'S INCREDIBLE PROMISE

1. Read through the verses from Romans chapter 8 below. As you read, make a list of all the promises God has made to us and all the things God says are true of us.

So now there is no condemnation for those who belong to Christ Jesus. . . . And Christ lives within you, so even though your body will die because of sin, the Spirit gives you life because you have been made right with God. . . . For all who are led by the Spirit of God are children of God. So you have not received a spirit that makes you fearful slaves. Instead, you received God's Spirit when he adopted you as his own children. Now we call Him "Abba, Father." For his Spirit joins with our spirit to affirm that we are God's children. . . .

And we know that God causes everything to work together for the good of those who love God and are called according to his purpose for them. For God knew his people in advance, and he chose them to become like his Son, so that his Son would be the firstborn among many brothers and sisters. And having chosen them, he called them to come to him. And having called them, he gave them right standing with himself. And having given them right standing, he gave them his glory.

What shall we say about such wonderful things as these? If God is for us, who can ever be against us? Since he did not spare even his own Son but gave him up for us all, won't he also give us everything else? . . .

Can anything ever separate us from Christ's love? Does it mean he no longer loves us if we have trouble or calamity, or are persecuted, or hungry, or destitute, or in danger, or threatened with death? . . .

And I am convinced that nothing can ever separate us from God's love. Neither death nor life, neither angels nor demons, neither our fears for today nor our worries about tomorrow—not even the powers of hell can separate us from God's love. No power in the sky above or in the earth below—indeed, nothing in all creation will ever be able to separate us from the love of God that is revealed in Christ Jesus our Lord.

2. Take one or more of the circumstances from the list you made in the "Make It Personal" section. How might the promises and truths from this section of Romans 8 affect your attitude and experience in these situations?

3. Can you thank God, not necessarily for the circumstances themselves, but for the promises He has made to you?

CHAPTER 3: IS EVERYTHING UNDER GOD'S CONTROL?

This chapter talks a lot about Satan and whether he is also under God's control.

1. What is Satan busy doing in the world now?

   Matthew 4:1; 13:19

   John 8:42–44

   Acts 5:3; 13:10

   2 Corinthians 2:11; 4:4; 11:3, 14–15

2. How is Satan under God's control, and what is his end?

   John 12:31; 16:8–11

Acts 26:18

1 John 3:8; 4:4

Revelation 20:10

3. Satan still has God's permission to send his fiery darts at us (Eph. 6:16), but God has provided us with full armor for our defense and battle. If the armor is in place, Satan cannot get through. What is this armor, and how does each piece enable us to repel Satan? See Ephesians 6:10–18.

4. How does God's truth (Eph. 6:14) help in effectively fighting against these common fiery darts?

Evil thoughts: James 1:12–14; 4:7

Depression: Psalm 27:13–14; 55:22; 103:13–14

Fears: Psalm 27:1; 56:3–4; 2 Timothy 1:7

CHAPTER 4: THE BIGGER PICTURE

1. How did God take what seemed only bad and turn it into something useful and beautiful for His purposes? We see three biblical characters whose bad situations God turned into good.

David: 2 Samuel 11:1–5; Psalm 51

Moses: Acts 7:22–36

Peter: Luke 22:54–62; John 21:15–17; Acts 2:22–24, 37–41

2. How did Paul see his imprisonment as part of God's bigger picture, which was working together for good?

Philippians 1:12–14

3. What can you learn from the examples above that you can apply to your own life when you struggle to see the bigger picture?

CHAPTER 5: BEING SURE OF GOD'S LOVING CONTROL

1. How can these verses help you respond to God's loving control? Write a key word or phrase for each response. Do you see any progression of responses?

1. 1 Peter 4:12

2. Jeremiah 11:5

3. Matthew 11:26

4. 2 Corinthians 12:10

5. James 1:2; Romans 5:3

6. Revelation 19:4, 6

2. Obviously we cannot actually see God in everything. We see Him by faith (2 Cor. 5:7). How do the following verses help us understand what this means?

Romans 4:20–21

2 Corinthians 4:16–18

Hebrews 11:1

3. Make notes from these verses on God's presence and involvement in our lives.

Exodus 33:14

Deuteronomy 31:6–8

Psalm 139:1–12

Jeremiah 23:23–24

John 14:16

Matthew 28:19–20

CHAPTER 6: DOES THIS END ALL OUR STRUGGLES?

1. How do these verses express God's promise to give the grace of endurance?

Isaiah 40:29–31

Philippians 1:6

Hebrews 12:1–3

James 1:2–4

1 John 5:4–5

2. From these verses, what can we look forward to in heaven?

Romans 8:17–18

1 Corinthians 2:9; 13:12

Hebrews 4:9–10

1 Peter 1:4

Revelation 21:3–4, 22–27; 22:3–5

3. How might looking forward to heaven change your perspective on your current struggles?

CHAPTER 7: WHY DO I FIND IT HARD TO TRUST GOD?

1. Is it possible to embrace the truth and still feel what you feel? How can you do this without denying your feelings?

2. Read Psalm 77. List some of the troubled feelings and questions that Asaph the psalmist expressed. Where does he begin to change his way of thinking about God? Can you trace how he reconciles his thinking?

3. Write out how you are currently feeling about your circumstances. Then follow Asaph's example in Psalm 77 and remind yourself of the ways God has shown His loving control for you in the past.

CHAPTER 8: GOD IS GOOD

1. Check out the revealed goodness of God in the following verses by writing the facts about Him stated there. How do we benefit from His goodness? (In some versions "goodness" is translated "lovingkindness.")

> Psalm 25:8–9; 33:5
>
> Matthew 6:30
>
> Acts 14:17

2. One possible reason we might not recognize God's love is that there is a blockage, a hindrance. Would you be willing to pray the prayer in Psalm 139:23–24? Ask the Holy Spirit to help you check it out as you read Isaiah 59:1–2, Micah 3:4, and Amos 3:3.

3. Is there some mysterious goodness of God affecting your life now? Write a sentence or two to God declaring your trust, even though you may not be able to make sense out of it in your present circumstances.

CHAPTER 9: UNOFFENDED BY THE UNEXPLAINED

1. Read Ruth 1:1–13, 20–21 and describe what God permitted to happen to Naomi. What did she conclude from what God had allowed (vv. 13, 20–21)?

> Read the rest of the book of Ruth to see how God redeemed her circumstances. Key verses: 2:8, 14–18; 4:13–17. Explain the difference in her circumstances at the end of the book.

2. Read Psalm 73. What was Asaph's first statement (v. 1)? But he had a problem. What seemingly unexplainable phenomenon was going on (vv. 2–3)?

What specific things had he noticed about the lives of the wicked (vv. 4–9)?

What helped him reconcile this seeming inconsistency in God's goodness (vv. 16–20)?

How does Asaph's response to God in verses 21–28 help us in our response when we are faced with frustrating, confusing, and seemingly unexplainable situations?

CHAPTER 10: WHAT PART DO I PLAY? AM I JUST A PASSIVE PUPPET?

1. From the following verses, discover why we need the Holy Spirit. We can't make it alone!

John 14:26

Romans 8:14–17, 26–27

1 Corinthians 12:4–11

Galatians 5:16, 22–23

2. Make a list of more truths about God and what He has done for us. Here are just a few examples to get you started:

Exodus 14:14

Romans 8:1

Romans 8:38–39

Ephesians 2:10

Philippians 1:6

CHAPTER 11: ATTITUDE, GRATITUDE

To help us develop an attitude of gratitude, we need to constantly remind ourselves of the following reasons we have to be thankful, regardless of our circumstances. Write out your responses.

1. Who God is

2. Who God says I am because of Christ

3. God's faithfulness as displayed in the Bible

4. God's faithfulness as displayed in my life

Draw the following table and take time now to add to each column. On an ongoing basis, review and remind yourself of the things you can be thankful for, and continue to add more.

Who God is	Who God says I am because of Christ	God's faithfulness as displayed in the Bible	God's faithfulness as displayed in my life

Use this table to help you express thanks to God.

Can you use this table to encourage others when they are struggling to be thankful?

CHAPTER 12: THE BOTTOM LINE

1. Although we cannot draw our security from people and things around us, what does Scripture tell us we should do for one another?

Galatians 6:2

Romans 12:9–18

1 Thessalonians 5:11–15

2. Ask yourself, what am I doing to help one other person mature in Christ? If you have no answer, pray that God will give you this opportunity with one person.

3. How will you continue to deepen your trust in the overarching truth of Romans 8:28 in your individual circumstances and as you try to help others?

References

CHAPTER 1   GOD KNOWS BEST

1   The foundation of this relationship with God is receiving Jesus Christ as your Savior from sin. The Bible tells us that everyone has sinned and cannot live up to God's standard of holiness. Romans 3:23 says, "For all have sinned and fall short of the glory of God." Romans 6:23 states, "For the wages of sin is death, but the gift of God is eternal life in Christ Jesus our Lord." This means that the penalty for our sins is death and an eternity without God (in hell). But there is good news! God sent His Son, Jesus Christ, to die in our place, taking the punishment that we deserve so we could be forgiven for our sins, spared from hell, and given eternal life and a relationship with Him. Romans 5:8 says, "But God demonstrates his own love for us in this: While we were still sinners, Christ died for us." According to the Bible, we aren't required to subscribe to a religious formula or do more good things than bad in the hope that we will find favor with God. No, God gives His gift freely to all who ask. "Everyone who calls on the name of the Lord will be saved" (Romans 10:13). Once you discover this and accept God's gift, the Bible says that you can be 100 percent assured of your eternal destination. 1 John 5:11–13 says, "And this is what God has testified: He has given us eternal life, and this life is in his Son.

Whoever has the Son has life; whoever does not have God's Son does not have life. I have written this to you who believe in the name of the Son of God, so that you may know you have eternal life." Furthermore, the Bible tells us of all the spiritual blessings that are true for each and every person once they accept God's gift. (Read Ephesians 1:1–14 to learn what some of these are.) Our prayer is that if you haven't already accepted God's gift, you will!

CHAPTER 2   GOD'S INCREDIBLE PROMISE

1   Jones, Jerry. "When It's Hard to Trust," *Virtue*, March/April 1985, 42.

2   See 1 Peter 5:10.

3   Jones, 42. Also recommend reading: Dr. Helen Roseveare, *Living Sacrifice*. Minneapolis: Bethany House Publishers, 1979.

CHAPTER 3   IS EVERYTHING UNDER GOD'S CONTROL?

1   See 2 Chronicles 20:6.

2   See Genesis 37–50.

3   See Matthew 4:1, Acts 5:3, 1 Peter 5:8, and Revelation 12:9.

4   See Job 1:13–19.

5   See Job 1:20.

6   See 1 John 4:4.

7   See Job 2:5–6.

8   See 2 Corinthians 12:7.

9   See 1 Corinthians 10:13, James 4:6–8, and 1 Peter 5:8–10.

10 Smith, Hannah Whitall. *The Christian's Secret of a Happy Life.* Old Tappan, NJ: Fleming H. Revell Company, 1952, 146.

11 See Psalm 37:1–8.

CHAPTER 4   THE BIGGER PICTURE: GOD'S MASTER PLAN

1   Chambers, Oswald. *My Utmost for His Highest.* New York: Dodd, Mead & Company, 1935, 25.

2   See Ephesians 3:20.

CHAPTER 5   BEING SURE OF GOD'S LOVING CONTROL
1   See Philippians 4:4–7.
2   See Romans 8:29.

CHAPTER 6   DOES THIS END ALL OUR STRUGGLES?
None

CHAPTER 7   WHY DO I FIND IT SO HARD TO TRUST GOD?
1   Smith, Hannah Whitall. *The God of All Comfort*. Chicago: Moody Press, 1973, 78–79.
2   See 1 Timothy 3:16 and Hebrews 1:3.

CHAPTER 8   GOD IS GOOD AND GOD IS LOVE
1   See 1 John 1:9 and Romans 8:35–39.
2   See Jeremiah 31:3.

CHAPTER 9   UNOFFENDED BY THE UNEXPLAINED
1   Elliot, Elisabeth. *On Asking God Why*. Old Tappan, NJ: Fleming H. Revell Company, 1989, 10.
2   See Psalm 103:13–14.
3   Yancey, Philip. *Where Is God When it Hurts?*, Marshall Pickering, 1998, 64.
4   See Psalm 18:2.
5   See John 13:7 and 21:20–22.

CHAPTER 10   WHAT PART DO I PLAY? AM I JUST A PASSIVE PUPPET?
1   Matthews, R. Arthur. *Born for Battle*. Robesonia, PA: OMF Books, 1978, 14.

CHAPTER 11   ATTITUDE, GRATITUDE
None

CHAPTER 12   THE BOTTOM LINE
1   Crabb, Lawrence J. *Basic Principles of Biblical Counseling*. Grand Rapids, MI: Zondervan, 1975, 65.

Order Information

To order additional copies of this book, please visit
www.redemption-press.com.
Also available on Amazon.com and BarnesandNoble.com
Or by calling toll-free 1-844-2REDEEM.